When Legacy Arises from the Thr
Collective of Trials and Tribulations Superseded by
Undeniable Victories
ISBN: 978-1-7341346-0-5

LOC Control #: 2019915904

Copyright © Brandi L. Rojas

Publisher and Editor: Fiery Beacon Publishing House

Fiery Beacon Consulting and Publishing Group

This work was produced in Greensboro, North Carolina,
United States of America.

When Legacy Arises from the Threshing Floor

A Collective of Trials and Tribulations Superseded by Undeniable Victories

Presented by

Brandi L. Rojas

And Twenty-Three

Powerhouse Literary Giants

Table of Contents

The Forward – Pastor Brandi L. Rojas

Section I: You Will Overcome the Abuse.

THE FORWARD

By Brandi L. Rojas

Blessings and Great Day to you and yours! My name is Brandi L. Rojas, and I serve as the Visionary Author and Publisher of this amazing project with these extraordinary women. Over these past months, I have had the opportunity to watch some go from crawling and others in isolation, all end up not flying but soaring.

There is something that happens when something breaks, and oftentimes the value of what is broken is revealed but the one who possesses it. I have experienced life and losses and to be honest heartbreak has accompanied more times than I care to count, but the Word of God reminds me of just how valuable a broken thing is. In Psalm 34:7 we find these words:

The LORD is near to the heartbroken And He saves those who are crushed in spirit (contrite in heart, truly sorry for their sin). (AMP)

This word could be no more true for me, and as you find, for these ladies as well. It was in what felt like the hardest of places that God not only showed up, but loved, consoled, comforted, empowered and led us on a powerful and relentless pursuit of wholeness. Even as I type these words I am reminded of my own brokenness and how God delivered.

When my father died and I wanted to take my life, rescue came. When foreclosure my dance studio came and I felt like I could not breathe, God sent a fresh wind to catapult my soul into purpose. When I experienced partial paralysis and felt completely bewildered, God confronted me with my call and further activated it in my life. As a prophet, when I began to feel the rejection from those I loved, even

9

some for my whole life, God sent His love to wipe my tears and restore me to a place of joy.

It was in places like these, that God showed Himself mighty and strong. Oftentimes, like the woman with the alabaster box, it does not make sense to worship through it, right? I mean, when life happens and pressures mount, no matter how "dedicated" we are, worship is not always our first response, but in those hours and even in this (whatever your "this" is), it is our greatest weapon.

Read each word intentionally. Read each word purposefully. Through these stories of testing, trial, tribulation and victory rest in knowing that whatever you have or will face —

NO WEAPON FORMED AGAINST YOU SHALL PROSPER. YOU ARE A SURVIVOR, A WINNER AND A CONQUEROR. THE VERY BREATH IN YOUR LUNGS IS THE VERY PROOF THAT YOU SURVIVED IT.

Now without further hesitation, in the words of my mentee, business partner and friend, Quashima Fisher who left this life in 2018 but never allowed her process to stop her purpose,

LET'S GET IT!

Pastor Brandi L. Rojas

Jesta Bouie

Jesta Bouie "Jes Speaking Truth" is a sought-after youth/women empowerment and motivational speaker against domestic violence for over 20 years, a high school teacher, assistant coach, mentor and wears many other hats within her local community, church and family. She is the mother of Travores, Talik and Malika and a native of Burlington N.C. who currently resides in Greensboro, NC. She a survivor of child abuse, neglect, molestation and domestic violence. She has been active in ministry for over 25 years and accepted her call into ministry in 2000. She is an ordained deaconess and minister of the gospel of Jesus Christ. After many years of running, she finally accepted and walks in her mantle as a prophetess (2018) under the leadership of Apostle Alicia Foust of Ignited Blue Apostolic Church International, Jamestown, N.C. She fully understands the plight of the rejected and the forgotten but knows that God has a purpose for everything.

May God continue to bless you!
Prophetess Bouie
Jesta "Jes Speaking Truth" Bouie

Jesta's Dedication

To God I give all the glory, honor and praise because if it had not been for Him who has always been on my side and continually guiding me, I truly do not know where I would be!

To Jessie Johnson Graves-my SuperGranny, until we meet again: the one who made me love to read books and told me that writing all of those book reports during all of my school breaks would pay off. Thank you for instilling the value of not just education but knowing the difference between wisdom and knowledge. You taught me how to use wisdom with all of the knowledge I have gained.

To my three heartbeats: Travores, Talik and Malika- thank you for always loving and pushing me. Travores thank you for always asking me, "What's REALLY wrong Ma? ", followed with one of your long hugs. Thank you for all of the real long talks about life, and most of all, the encouragement you have not just given to me in action and love but the words that you spoke as my oldest to me and your brother and sister. Talik, thank you for always being my laughter- the one who has a way of making me bust out laughing by something that you do. Most of all thank you for your raw and completely honesty when it comes to how you see life. Malika, the one they all call my mini-me, I could write a book just on you and it would be a best-seller. Thank you, my little genius of a blessing, for being who you are in my life, my last child with so much talent and joy. Thank you for all the questions, kisses, hugs, long crazy car rides and mommy and daughter dates. To my children, I love all of you to life and God have me 3 life lines to make sure that I lived even on the days I truly did not want to go on- thank you for being the PUSH, PULL, the NUG and the reason to continue to push through this thing called LIFE! With God and you three always beside, in front of and

12

behind me there will always be something for me to achieve!

To Lynette Carter, the first person who spoke BOOKS into my life out of my belly. The words that you spoke over me at your women's gathering that day was life changing in more ways than you knew at the time. You told me to not just tell my life story but to write out my LIFE because the life that I had lived so far was going to give LIFE to others. I did not understand it then, but I do now.

To My mentor/leader and master teacher, Apostle Alicia Foust thank you for catapulting me into becoming me. #IAMSHE #QUEENME #HERMAJESTY.

Love,

Jesta

Connect with Jesta:

Email: jesblessedprofessionalservices@gmail.com

Business Phone: (540) 214-1317 cell

CHAPTER 1

Forgiving Without Apologies

By Jesta Bouie aka ~ Jes Speaking Truth Boldly

"HE TOUCHED ME- MOMMY HE TOUCHED ME!"

As I ran out the house at the age of 8 years old, I prayed that the woman who watched me sometimes was home and that her front screen door was open. All I needed to do was to call Ma (Granny) and tell her that I needed her to come get me. Would she believe me? What was I going to say when she answered the phone because Ma was always home in the morning time? I was running as fast as my fat little short feet can take me and thinking, "Ma you told me to always pray because God hears all little children's prayers! All I could think about was all the times you told me to just bow my head and talk to God as if I was talking to you. Well, I have been bowing my head and talking but I really do not think that God has or can hear me. God, were you listening when he walked in the bathroom and just looked at me and smiled knowing that he was going to do it again? God, did you see him touching and feeling on me in places that my teacher said no one should touch? 'Him' loves to tell mommy to leave me here because she is just going to the store and I have to finish reading that book, except this time, I am going to finish reading this book!" I told her last time when he grabbed me and sat me on his lap, that he touched me, and it made me feel nasty. I told her that he made me touch places that I did not like to touch. Mommy, I told you, but you said, 'no he did not touch you like that.' I was told that my imagination was grand! So, I ran and called granny, my superhero, because I knew that if I told her that she would come and make him STOP. As I ran in the lady's house after busting through her storm door, I asked, "Can I please call my granny?" I rattled off the number and she dialed it and gave me the phone. Ma answered and I told her to please come get me or I was going to run away and go the train or bus station. I instructed her to come to Pine St. because he had hit me and touched me. My granny replied, "I believe you and I coming to get you!" Before the lady could say anything, and after I laid phone down, I ran out the house and back home and when I saw that he was still asleep I grabbed my blanket, pillow, and baby doll and hid in the back closet in the hope chest and quietly hummed! I could hear so much going on around me, but I just hummed! "Where is she?" I could smell him in the room where I was hiding but he could not hear me humming because he still had the music playing in the next room. I could hear the cars passing by the house, but I was only listening for the sound of one of three cars that I could remember. My uncle's car had a funny sound when the backdoor was being closed, rather slammed shut. My granddad's car was quiet, but you could hear the motor "purr" as all the old men in the family would say. When my granny got out of a car, she had a silent walk but with the power behind it, you could hear her when one of her grands needed her. I heard couple of cars pull up and one I did not notice the sound of. I heard the old man a few houses down hollering at his dogs to shut up. I heard the train coming from across town. The clock on the wall was just ticking too slow today for me. Then I heard as loud but so softly in my ear what he would always say after he did what he did each time, "Nobody is going to believe you and if they do it will kill your beloved granny! I ain't scared of your family!" Just as she came home, my Calvary army arrived. All I can remember is my mother saying, "She's lying again! She keeps on lying and I am going to beat her a** for lying Ma!" My granny backhanded my mother so hard that she hit the wall. My uncles were on a rampage for real; I always called them the quiet before the storm because they both were very quiet men but a deadly force to be reckon with. This time was different, I could hear both of them talking very clearly as they were coming into the house.

One said, "just shut up and stop telling lies. That baby ain't got no reason to lie. Now where in the hell is he? You gone take this beating for him? Please get out the way! Where is Shon?" It was like watching a 3D fighting scene in slow motion on high-definition television and those had not even been thought of back then. So, after the fight scene that my eyes to this day can still visualize in slow motion, my auntie along with my granny gathered my belongings and told my mommy to not even think about trying to get me back because it was not happening. This day made it abundantly clear, that she had decided that a man was more important than believing her only child who happened to be a little girl. With big crocodile tears in my eyes, I prayed that my mother would not die because of the look of hurt on her face after all that had transpired. Both of my uncles' hands were bleeding and swollen because of the way they both kept on punching, hitting and throwing him around like a ragdoll and any and everything that was in their path. They looked horrible and were very upset. I was safety buckled in the backseat and going back to my hometown and a safe haven.

HUH LORD! REALLY?

"Forgive her, NOW!" Forgive your mother NOW!" "You must forgive here NOW!" These were the words attached to the loud and powerful small still voice that spoke to me. I was taken back and could not say anything but, "HUH, Lord, really!" I was so upset that I immediately felt like I was going to pass completely out. "God are you serious? REALLY, right now at this moment? I have to get up and deliver this sermon that you called me to do TODAY!" God's response was not what I thought it would be. "Daughter, my child, I died for the forgiveness of ALL of mankind SINS and everyone has not told me that they are sorry! I died so that you may live!"

I took a deep breath and said, "God she never said she believed me and it was true. He did it and she stayed.

17

God she stayed and helped him raise his child! She called his only daughter her child and forgot that she had me. I am her only child. She abused me as a child and lied about it. She is the reason that my biological father could never really have a relationship with me because of all of the crazy things she had not only said but done! I was homeless teenage mother my senior in high school because she smoked up the rent money. To add fuel to the fire, she lied to people about me needing things during the process of the family burying Mama Jessie. I had to go in a trap house to get my first born, her first grandchild, because she could not stay sober long enough to watch him. This was after everyone in the family told me to give her a chance because she was my mother. I wrote her a letter years ago telling her that I forgave her for everything and stated how proud I was of her for being off crack cocaine for years. Lord, what else could I do? Every time I forgive her, she does something else! God, I let her have a relationship with my children, her only grandchild and she has messed that up. I had to go get Vores from a traphouse in Winston-Salem and he was less than a year old. I was obedient when you told me to let her stay with me when I moved back to B-ton after Talik was born. She stole clothes from her own grandkids and tried to sell them to her niece-REALLY God!? I almost lost a car because one of her many boyfriends stole it and tried to sell it for some CRACK!

God said it again, *"Forgive her, NOW!" Forgive your mother NOW!" "You must forgive her NOW! You did not need an apology from her! Did I not answer your prayer of saving her life when she was shot? You prayed and every time I showed you visons of things happening with her laying in a pool of blood, standing and bullets flying all around her, visions of her heart busting out of her chest in a room, etc."*

"Okay", I replied, "I hear you; this is too much to bear right now! My heart felt like it was going to bust out

18

of my chest and fall in the floor. I bowed my head and repented to God for having so much bitterness, hatred, malice and just downright conditional love in my heart towards my mother. I had loved her just because everyone had been telling me that she was my mother and I should love her. To top it off, they loved to throw the commandment of "honor thy mother and father so that thee days will be long" in my face. As tears fell from my eyes, I asked God to forgive me for not forgiving her and I prayed and told my mind, my heart, my soul and the inner part of me to forgive her. I walked up to her as she walked towards me in the church and as I hugged her; I told that I forgave her, and I loved her. She had a crazy look on her face, but I knew I had truly released her in my heart because I felt such a weight lift off me. I was very light-headed, and my ears popped loud from the inside. I thought that I would not be able to hear for a minute until I heard God said, "***Thank you daughter and now watch what I do in you because you truly know what forgiveness is all about! You forgiving her was not just for her but for you!***"

I was able to minister in a way that I had never spoken before. The church was packed out that day with kids, youth and women of all ages. One of my co-workers who I had become very close friends with had come to hear me and she bought all of her kids. She told me after the service that two of five kids never really paid attention in church but they both hung onto every word that came out of my mouth. They both ended up have a very long talk with her a few weeks later and was working on restoring broken relationship in their family.

I learned that day standing in that church what true forgiveness felt like and that sometimes we must forgive without an apology or explanation. I untied God's hands in my life, and I thank Him for forgiving me daily. I am able to tell so many others that it is just not a commandment to honor your parents, but we must forgive them to with and without apologies. We must understand that we do not chose who our parents are, but God does and he NEVER makes a mistake. No one is perfect on this Earth or in this entire world, but a mother's love is a love that no one can take away. I can only speak and understand a child or children who's mother did not raise, fully raise or finish raising them. Children must get to a point in their lives where God cannot just teach them but they can see what unconditional love is and how forgiveness is a must. Forgiveness without an apology or apologies release you from things all of the things that have been weighing you down (bitterness, hatred, jealously, misunderstanding, negative thoughts, etc.) for God's greatness and all of the fruit of the spirit to come into your life. One thing I did learn from forgiving without an apology is that it released me to help reach, not just my destiny, but my purpose in the kingdom of God and in life. It untied God's hands, made the pathway clear for me to receive blessings that had been held up for years and released and broke things within my bloodline so that children would not have to deal with or fight against it. I can freely be the vessel that God chose to use for the kingdom, in the kingdom and in daily life to help others see and know that forgiveness can be accomplished and done! True forgiveness is a release in your heart and being where God steps in and gives you unconditional love.

Laura Brown Spencer

Laura Brown Spencer is the daughter of Bishop Larry & Mother Elsie Brown and the firstborn of six children. She is the mother of three amazing girls. She has five sweet grandchildren and two adorable great-grandchildren. She is a high school graduate. She worked at Quality Mills and Blue Bell. She is a retired Instructional Assistant Teacher at Southern Pines Primary School. She has been an Instructional Assistant's Teacher of the Year, A distributor for Total Life Changes and an Executive Vice President of Network Marketing of Keys to Building Wealth which she does from home.

She is a person who loves the Lord and attends church at the House of Prayer, The Holy Church of God in Christ. She has been a Church Secretary, President of the Choir, President of the Ushers Board of The Holy Churches of God in Christ and a member of Taylortown Community Choir.

She loves to travel. She has traveled to Jamaica, Mexico, Antigua, Cayman Islands, Barbados, Key West Florida, Puerto Rico and the Bahamas.

Her goal is to travel and be a motivational speaker for the Lord.

Laura's Dedication

I dedicate this book to God, for I have dedicated my life to him. He is the author and finisher of my Life.

My parents Bishop Larry and Mother Elsie Brown, who gave birth to me, raised me to the best of their ability and introduced me to Jesus Christ.

My daughters, Tiphanie Drakeford, Shereka Lindsey and Keyana Drakeford whom I raised as a single parent and introduced them to Christ then ended up being a direct recipient of their prayers for me through all of my hurt and pain. They gave great support along with my parents, while I was going through the process of this part of my journal.

Prophetess Vivian Brown, who recognized the cry for help. She put forth Romans 15:1 into action. We who are strong are to bear the infirmities of the weak. She did not know how to come to me, so she reached out to my daughter, Keyana, to talk to me to find out what they need to pray for.

My sister Janet Brown, who told me about a class that she felt might help me through my hurt, pain, anger, and bitterness.

My former pastor, Pastor Jerome Williams who said, "you need to just start where you are in Christ and build back up your relationship with Him." Also, his wife First Lady Nancy Williams who said to me that "sometimes you have to just work on you."

My aunt Vickie Kelly and the Greater Glory Church gave me a platform to talk about Transitioning with a Purpose.

My brother Phillip Brown who often tells me to write down the vision and make it plain and watch it come into a reality.

Alcott Spencer who came into my life and made my dream a reality.

Larry Drakeford for my amazing girls and putting me in the position to realize I am a strong woman. I did not need a man to raise children; with God's help, I did survive.

Pastor Jones who prophesied over me and told me to "Go ahead and write that book you already started on."

Connect with Laura:
www.facebook.com/laura.spencer.520
www.linkedin.com/in/laura-spencer0b8853146
www.youtube.com/user/lauraspencer54.

CHAPTER 2:
Stepping out of the Norm and Into My Destiny

Growing up in a Christian household had its ups and downs. Being a P.K. (Preacher's Kid) we were to walk what they called, "the chalk line." While being a child you do not always know what adults mean by what they say; sometimes you just want to be a regular kid. You just want to go to the movies, ball games, become a girl scout or brownie. Being a P.K., sometimes the answer was **NO**, and that answer often left me wondering why other kids could do certain activities that I could not do; it made no sense. I always felt that maybe those kids were better than me. When the students came to school and talked about what a good time they had and I had nothing to say, I felt disconnected.

I never understood why even the kids at our church could go to these activities! Why were we the only ones in church, bored, tired and unable to finish our homework because we had so much to do? Back then the saints believed that *me and my household are going to serve the Lord*. (Boy, they sure did believe that saying!) It is kind of comical now. When revival time came around, we knew they were going to call us up to the mourner's bench. We would cringe in our seat when all the saints turned around and looked at all the children. We were made to go up and sit on the front pew to listen to the sermon. We did not hear him, because we did not want to be put on the spot of pretending to be something we did not know how to be. When he was finished preaching, they would pull out those single chairs right in front of the front pew, so you were facing the audience. We would get on our knees with our buns held tight and shaking because we were afraid that they would begin singing over us; we wanted to get up and

25

leave but could not. They would stomp and pat their hands for what seemed like all night. They would tell us to tell the Lord to save us while spitting on us, not intentionally of course. In our minds, we were not ready to be saved; we did not know what it all meant.

They would sing for hours and hours and hours. The word was passed down for me to get up and shout. "Ok", I would say. I would get up to start shouting and the rest would join me so we all would say "thank you, Jesus!" Once we said that, they would stop singing and we could finally go home. Yes, we would dance when the music was good and sometimes, we "felt the spirit", but when we heard Teenage Frolic music the following Saturday we started dancing to the worldly music and when the next spring came we had to be saved all over again. We repeated the same procedure until we were sixteen. By then we would have jobs and when revival came around the following spring, we could decide to go to church or work, so we chose work.

By the age of sixteen, I heard the word **No** way too often: "**No**, you cannot have a car! **No**, you cannot go to the movies! **No**, you cannot date! **No**, you cannot have a job working in tobacco! **No**, you do not need that job, it will take you away from the church!" Wow, here we go again - "others can but we cannot." I began to think everything cannot be a **No**, so I started doing my own thing. A job came up where I could babysit for my family. I was keeping roughly ten kids for ten dollars a kid a week which was a hundred dollars a week. Wow, I can buy school clothes and help my parents out! So, I began to do the job for my family, until I was molested. Molestation turns a woman's life upside down. It takes away your dignity and makes you feel worthless and ugly. Molestation comes to take everything that is

26

good away from you. Most people do not tell others they have been molested or raped because of the people who will not believe them or blame them for flirting in front of the molester even when it never happened that way. I felt let down again, so I entrusted it to someone I felt would do something about it but unfortunately, they did not.

When a person is hurt it sticks with them for a long time. During this time in my life, I said, "maybe they do not know what to do so they do nothing hoping it will go away." The truth is it never goes away. Sometimes it still hurts, because you cannot believe that someone could have the heart to do such a thing. So, I went to the Creator who created me and him; still, nothing was done so it remained in the back of my mind until the molester targeted the next victim. It was not until the molester had another victim that something was done, leaving me feeling that my case was not worthy enough to have justice served. Knowing that my offender was now imprisoned, I began to go forward with my life with the approach that what happened would never happen again until someone said, "Look at that body! If you weren't close to me I would do it to you too." That comment disgusted me so much that I began to neglect my appearance; I no longer wanted the fine curves they were after. I felt as if my "fine body" was causing me to fall victim to bad things.

So, life proceeded, and I started dating and eventually found out that I was expecting a child. I was ok with that since I was not allowed to go away to college and felt I could handle the two; being and raising a child felt difficult, but with the help of my baby's father I knew there was no way that I could lose. (I figured, at least my parents' relationship with six kids was working so I would definitely be ok.) I was proposed to by the father of the baby which sounded like a good idea; we loved each other, have a child together and now we were going to be a complete family. I was happy until we had to share the money for the bills. I was willing to pay bills just not by myself. I knew that is what we had to do to survive as a family. My husband was no longer working, not because he was laid off, but because he had pretended to go to work, and got fired for not going to work; maybe he was not taught that you work and pay bills together.   Money is a major factor that has the capacity to destroy a marriage. Some people do not think about the long haul, but instead, only consider the present. Marriage is supposed to last forever but for some, sadly, it does not.

I found myself stuck with raising my child alone but willing to do whatever it took to raise them. What happens when you are trying to please God and trying to keep your marriage with a partner who wants to be free? Even in places like this, God may not come when you expect, but He will come, so I waited. I had two more children by the same man because I was a sexual person and I could not go to anyone else even if I wanted to; he was my husband and I was waiting on God to turn him around so we could live like a saved family. I stayed with him through his drunkenness, cheating, the beating and not supporting his family. The members of the church would give their stories of how God worked it out for them through some of the same situations. I tried it, thinking that if they could overcome it so could I. This situation drove me to my knees; I fasted and prayed so much that one night I started hyperventilating until I passed out on the floor. This situation drained me naturally and spiritually; I felt like all hope was gone.

I remember another time - I was praying for while waiting for this one to be answered and told God that I was tired of praying repeatedly for the same things and that I could not do it anymore. I thought about how I was molested and prayed for my marriage to no resolve. I felt that if God did not care, no one else would. I found myself saying, "God I am your child, why am I getting treated like this?" I began to feel worthless. I heard one preacher say, "some folks are tagged for hell", and began thinking that I must have been one of them because I could not get any prayers answered, especially the ones I thought God would answer. I was so heartbroken. When we went to events and outings with the church, I was always alone with my children with no husband around. I felt like an outcast at school and at church. I hated Women's Day at church because they would talk about how to treat your husband when, in my case, their words had nothing to do with my situation, so I would sit in my seat with a broken heart in silence, not knowing what to do. I asked God to let me cry on the inside so the saints would not see how broken I was. They did not know that I cried myself to sleep almost every night; it was so embarrassing.

I often heard the testimonies of people who were still waiting or had not received the answer they wanted from the prayers they prayed; the saints would listen to me tell some of my stories and reply with "Oh ye of little faith!" or "If your mother could see you now they would be so proud that you have given yourself to the Lord." I wondered if I would be among the number of those who prayed with all of their hearts only to have their prayer be answered after they passed away because I did not have enough faith. How would that ever benefit me? In my mind, I had resolved that it would just be something else that would be packed away in my wondering broken heart.

Fourteen years later of struggling as a single parent, I heard a sermon about having faith in God and trusting Him to do the work; the Lord had blessed me with my own brand-new mobile home and a brand-new car all in the same year. I finally felt like God heard me and that the prayer of my husband being saved would finally be answered. So, I tried praying again only to find out the answer was still silence. I could not go through the same scenario again, so I decided to take that prayer request and tuck it in the back of my mind; to think that it would again go unanswered was too much pain to bear.

Time progressed and with three children, I started working two jobs so I could keep a roof over our heads, food in our home and transportation for our family. The press was rewarding and allowed me to handle our needs with a little leftover for fun moments too. I had the opportunity to cruise to different foreign countries and had a great time learning about different cultures and the different ways they expressed worshipping God. It was an exciting experience.

One night, I dreamed about a lot of greenery going up a hill; someone was chasing me up that hill and I was laughing and having so much fun. I ran until I came to a white house and a rose bush. There was a group of people who favored me. I dreamed that I was at the bridge with this group of people; I did not know what happened but somehow, I fell off a bridge. I never hit rock bottom because I would always wake up. When you dream the same dream four times doing the same thing, you begin to wonder why. Just when you stop thinking about it the dream comes to life in a way you never expect.

A group of people came to work for a hotel where I used to work my second job. These people favored me because they said I was not "fake." I would act the same way towards them no matter what. There was a guy in this group who wanted to talk to me and get more acquainted. Thinking that everyone could use a good friend, we began our friendship. I was still in a place in my life where God was not answering me; I was going to church, praising God, and even got the group of people to come to church with me. One day a guy from that group called my second job. The boss came to get me and said, "you are wanted on the phone." Immediately, my motherly instinct set in. I thought maybe something happened at home, and my girls were calling wanting to know what to do in a tough situation. (My girls were no longer babies; they had jobs and had even purchased cars at this time.)

When I got to the phone it was a guy from the group with a West Indian accent wanting to know if I was going anywhere the next day, and that he would like to come along to see what the United States had to offer. In my opinion, there was no harm in that, especially since I had a lot to do the next day. I had to go out of town and thought it would be good to have another person go with me. By then, I had worked with him for about three months and he seemed to be a nice guy, so I picked him up and off we went. Though we were becoming more acquainted, I still considered our relationship to be purely platonic; regardless of my perception he wanted more.

One evening everything changed. I got on my knees and prayed that God would remove him if he was not for me; during my prayer he called my phone. It seemed as if God was not going to remove him and since we had to see one another at work the situation could not be avoided. Things between us progressed quickly until suddenly, one day he proposed. I initially told him no, but that did not stop him. He would always go home in December and return in March, so the calls kept coming but this time from the Caribbean Islands. By this time, I began falling for him. In my eyes, he had now become something I did not have but would love to have in my life. Upon his return in March it had become obvious that his feelings for me never changed. At the end of the season he proposed for a second time and again my answer was no, but by the third proposal that answer swiftly changed into a YES! There was never a time where I felt like ending what was happening between us or considered the reality of my relationship with God.

I was already divorced and had been separated for twenty-four years or more; I began to think of all the times I prayed to God about my first marriage and nothing was done. I was beaten, cheated on and not provided for but my new husband provided for me and he did not beat me. He made sure I was well taken care of until I found out he was cheating on me too. "Oh no not another cheater!" I thought. Something happened and he was deported back to Jamaica. I went there several times; my last time in Jamaica, I was sitting on the porch with my laptop and I heard God say, "look up." I looked up and saw nothing. He said it again a second time; it was not until I heard the words "look up" for the third time that I stopped and waited for God to speak. He said, "look in front of you", and my dream unfolded right before my very eyes - the greenery, the hill I was running on when I was chased in my dream, the white house and the rose bush even the group of people who favored me were all accounted for. I cried and said, "I am here".

Something in me felt like this journey of my life was coming to an end. Now I understood the dream. Sometimes the plans we think are for us are not the plans God has for us. My husband could not live the American dream he wanted because he was deported and I could not have a husband like I always wanted, because he cheated, and did not want to adapt to his Jamaican lifestyle. I was hanging on by a thread, but no one knew because I keep my feelings hidden. On the other hand, I was so tired of things not working in my life. I told God I was not going to pray anymore. As I was turning in my driveway I started praying again. I got a little upset because I could not keep my word. My burden was so heavy, I could not lift my hands to give God praise. I could not say "Hallelujah"; it would not flow freely. I found myself angry, bitter, hurt and in pain. I was so fed up until it started to spill over. I could no longer hide my pain my hurt anymore. I was hurting people who were close to me because I was hurting. I was not hurting them intentionally; it was happening because I had packed all of the pain down on the inside of me instead of getting healed and delivered. I kept feeling like no one really cared. God could solve this problem, but why had He not done it yet?

I stopped caring about myself. I could no longer sing like I used to because I was singing through anger and pain. When I talked to people, they could hear it in my voice. I was crying out for help, but no one could recognize it. People felt like I was just being mean, but I had never been a mean person. I thank God for the Prophetess at our church who used my daughter to connect with me to see why I was so unhappy; I am grateful for the day they began to pray together on my behalf. Galatians 6:2 says, **"Bear ye one another burdens and so fulfill**

the law of Christ." I thank God for my daughters who I introduced to Jesus Christ who, in return, prayed that I would get back on track. My daughters said, "Mom, I think you are bitter from all of the things life has put you through." My sister listened to me and brought me a Great Commission booklet from the church she attended. There was a class offered that was open to the public, so I decided to attend. I asked God to help me because I knew it was never my intention to hurt anyone; what hurt even more was the fact that I kept doing what my heart did not want to do to the people I loved.

I kept praying. In bible study at my local church, we were reading the book of Matthew 5:32 about being divorced and what was to be expected; everyone wanted to know why I remarried. God, at that time, would not let me say anything. My mind became discombobulated and my brain felt like scrambled eggs to the point where I could hear the sizzling in my head. One of my daughters saw what I was going through and felt that I was being attacked. I went home and prayed some more. I said, "Lord now that I have sinned against you, I am now being called an adulterer. I have caused my second husband to be called one as well. Have I lost out on heaven?" I was feeling low, like knee-high to a grasshopper. I cried until the Lord spoke to me and said, "Are not all sins forgiven?" My former pastor said, "You have to start where you are in Christ". I stopped in my tracks when God spoke and Jeremiah 1:5 came to mind.

"Before I formed thee in the belly, I knew thee; and before thou cameth forth out of the womb, I sanctified thee, and I ordained thee a prophet unto the nation."

I said, "Wait one minute," - I had to talk to myself while God was talking to me. I thought about the dream and how it was revealed to me and how I fell off the bridge in my dream but did not hit the ground. I might have fallen off the tracks a little bit, but it only takes a spark to keep the fire going. **Proverbs 22: 8** says,

"Train up a child in the way it should go, and when he is old, he will not depart from it,"

That seed that was planted inside of me started to bloom again; the roots were already there but needed a little nourishing. I grabbed hold of faith and stepped out of the Norm of "No" into my Destiny of "Yes." **Habakkuk 2:2-3** says:

"Write the vision and make it plain upon the tables; that he may run he who readeth it. For the vision is for an appointed time, but at the end, it shall speak, and not lie. though it may tarry wait for it will surely come, and not tarry."

My brother often reminds me of this scripture. I wrote down my own affirmation and motivation of faith; I knew that I had to write the vision and make it plain and would have read to it until it became a reality. Here are a few scriptures that I used to begin speaking destiny to myself.

I can do all things through Christ who hath strengthen me.   **- Philippians 4:13**
Faith is the substance of things hoped for, the evidence of things not seen.

- Hebrews 11:1
Ask and it shall be given you: seek and ye shall find: knock and it shall be opened unto you. For everyone that asketh receiveth and he that seeketh findeth;

and to him that knocketh it shall be opened.

- Matthew 7:7-8

If ye shall ask anything in my name, I will do it.

- Matthews 19:26

With men, this is impossible, with God all things are possible.   **- John 14:14**

For God has not given us a spirit of fear, but of power and of love and of a sound mind.

- 2 Timothy 1:7

This process took me from a seed to a root, to a leaf and ultimately a full-grown plant. With these scriptures, I am   **Stepping out of the Norm and Into my Destiny.**

I am finished with this chapter of my life; I am stepping out of the negative mindset and adopting a positive mindset that will serve as my GPS to my destiny. Watch out devil is going to be rough tackling me in this next chapter of my life! God has something He wants me to do and I am created for that purpose. I realize it a process. With God on my side I am going to make it, and to my readers, so will you.

Mary Holman

Mary Holman was born and raised in Cleveland, Ohio by two wonderful parents, Willie L. and Princella Davis. She is the youngest of four children and was a Daddy's girl.

She attended several elementary schools while growing up in Cleveland - Mary B Martin, Sowinski, and finally John W Raper, where she graduated and went on to Lula Dahl Junior High, which was a very popular all-girls school at that time. After graduating from middle school, she attended East High School, home of The Bombers, and graduated at the age of 17 on the B Honor Roll with a 3.5 grade average.

She married her high school sweetheart who had joined the Airforce while she was in her junior year that allowed her to see the world. The assignments took her to many places including CCK AFB in Taiwan and Tyndal AFB, Panama City, Florida where she had her first daughter Nikki and 18 months later her second daughter Kenyada. Next, was Langley AFB in Hampton Virginia for six years where she worked as an admissions clerk in the Trauma center and attended Sunrise Vocational School for Nursing. They were then sent to Sembach AFB in Sembach Germany, where she had her last two daughters, Christine and Yolanda.

After the three-year tour there, they were given orders to Nellis AFB in Las Vegas Nevada, where she presently resides. Four daughters and 18 grandchildren later, she has become a Chaplain for the State of Nevada, a certified relationship coach and now a best-selling author.

Her mission is to bring hope to the hopeless, let them know that there are people out here who really care and that they do not have to remain a victim; they can become the victor. She wants people to know that Christianity is not about legalism or religion – it is about a Relationship with Christ.

Her future plans are to write several books, travel in ministry and help others.

Mary's Dedication

To my Heavenly Father, who loved me beyond measure: Through every storm that I endured, He was right there. His unfailing love is what kept me, protected me, shielded me and comforted me through the pain and the sleepless nights. I owe Him my life and I gladly give it to Him. I Thank you Father that you did not allow the enemy to triumph over me.

To my parents, who have now gone to be with the Lord: I thank them for raising me in the love and admonition of the Lord. They were very nurturing, caring, supportive, providers, protectors, entrepreneurs who owned not only one but two businesses, Davis Dry Cleaners and Gulf Gas Station. They were very hard workers, and in spite of it all they still found time for family. They kept us in church and taught us how important Integrity is. I will forever be grateful to them for all that they have done for me, and for loving me through thick and thin.

To the four jewels of my life, my daughters, Nikki Scott, Kenyada Smith, Christine Campbell and Yolanda Whitehead: I dedicate this book to you, because you were there through my storms. You prayed with and for me and never gave up on me; you continue to love me, have faith in me, and believe the best for me. I could not have made it without you neither could I have asked for anyone better than you guys. You hold the four chambers of my heart and I love you from here to Eternity.

To Pastor Brandi Rojas: Thank you for this opportunity, because the things that she required of me gave me insight about things that I did not see in myself, but now I do. You helped me to see that I am not a reject, I am a valuable commodity, and I am learning my self-worth. I salute you; you brought healing to this chapter of my life.

Last but not least, I dedicate this book to all of the survivors of domestic abuse.

Connect with Mary
Website: www.bustercoco.neora.com

Phone: (702) 205-1330

CHAPTER 3

Forgiveness is my Crown

There are at least 20 people per minute that are physically abused by an intimate partner or spouse. I became one of the statistics. Abuse is real and it has many faces; there is physical abuse, verbal abuse, mental abuse, emotional abuse, sexual abuse, psychological abuse, rejection, neglect, and manipulation. I am sure there are probably more. I experienced several of them. The Washington Post states that half of the women that were murdered in the past decade were murdered by either past or present intimate partners and that is where my relationship was heading. I went through a lot of hurt and pain before I realized I deserved better, and that I was worth much more than I realized. It is sad to think that, if you never realize your worth, you will allow the cycle to continue even into the next relationship. We are a valuable commodity in the eyes of God and that is the way we should be treated by the man or woman that say they love us. There were several red flags that I saw and ignored - after all I was young and in love.

We had been in the relationship for about three years before we married. I remember him telling me about a girl that he dated and how they had gotten into an argument and he beat her while she was crossing the street. He laughed and thought it was funny and I did not think anything of it; this was red flag number one. The second red flag was when we were invited to his mother's house for dinner and I did not like cornbread; he insisted that I taste his mother's cornbread and I refused, so he tried to shove it in my mouth. I got mad but after he apologize everything was ok. Abuse begins very subtle and starts with small things that we overlook or ignore. if we continue to allow it to happen it could possibly cost us our lives.

I was fifteen years old and just coming out of junior high when I met him. My brother had become friends with Lee and wanted him to teach him how to play the bass guitar. He was over to the house almost every day, and after a while it was almost like he was family, so much so that he even joined us on a family vacation to Tuskegee, Alabama. At first, he pretended to ignore me, but after a few days we began to tease and flirt with each other, especially when mom and dad were not around. Shortly after getting back home we started dating. He was the love of my life. We dated for almost two years before he got a letter from the government for him to be drafted into the Army, but instead of going to the Army, he decided to sign up for the Air Force. By now, I was a junior in high school, and I will never forget the day he left; I felt like my world was falling apart. We had a good relationship; we had never had sex and he was determined to wait until I felt that I was ready. We wrote each other almost every day, and in between the letters he would call two to three times a week. After being away for a while, the letters slowed down and the calls were less frequent, but, since he was not stationed that far, he began to come home on the weekends. It was on one of those occasions that I decided I was ready. He was shocked, but I realized if I did not sleep with him and do something soon, he might meet someone else that would capture his attention while he was away.

So here we are: the very first time we decided to have sex, I got pregnant, at the age of seventeen. I was scared and excited at the same time, because I was in love with him and we had already talked about getting married someday. When I was four months pregnant, I confided in my sister, who betrayed me by telling my mom who then told my dad. I was a daddy's girl, I was his heart, and now I had broken it.

42

You know, back in those days you were expected to graduate from high school, go to college, find a good job, get married and have a nice family. So naturally, my father was very upset with me, told me to call Lee, tell him I was pregnant and that he needed to send for me. That was the first time I had ever really felt rejection from my father. Reluctantly, I did as my father said and called Lee hoping he would be happy, but instead, he was angry, began to say it was my fault, that I was messing up his life and he did not have anywhere for me to stay. This became the second time that I felt the devastating pain of rejection by the one that was supposed to love me the most. I felt confused, lost, and abandoned. It was only the grace of God that kept me from losing my mind. My mom had some choice words of her own that were like daggers in my heart as well. I was already feeling like crap, and she made it even worse. After a while, I found myself talking back to her, which was something I had never done, but I was hurt and did not know what to do.

Lee had suggested that I have an abortion, but that was the furthest thing from my mind. My mother convinced him that it would be the best thing to do since we were still young and had our whole lives ahead of us, and he agreed. I was heartbroken, but since I was underage, she had the right, at that time, to make the decision to terminate the pregnancy. Since I was so far along, I had to have the procedure done in the hospital and stay overnight. I had the surgery that morning and later that afternoon, he called saying, "Since you had it done, it must not have been my baby". Being emotionally distraught already, I cannot remember my response, but it was nothing pretty. I was pissed off! I had never felt that angry before, so I broke up with him. As I look back, I am grateful to God that He kept me from suicidal thoughts and deep depression. I continued going to school and graduated the following year; life was good. Lee, in the meantime, continued to call me and would

43

come home periodically and stay at the house with my brother. I felt this was a way for him to get back with me, and despite what had happened, I still loved him and eventually we got back together. A few months, later I went to be with him in Utah where he was stationed.

One day while we out, we stopped by one of his friend's house. When we went inside, I sat in the living room, as they were busy talking and walking towards the kitchen. I sat there for a few minutes and when I looked towards the kitchen, I saw him roll up his sleeve and tie a rubber band around his arm while another guy stood there with a spoon holding a lighter under it to melt whatever was inside. The guy took the needle and drew the substance, which I later found out was heroin, and proceeded to inject it into Lee's arm. I was in shock; I could not believe it! This was not what I expected when I decided to leave home to be with him. I told him I was going back home, but he convinced me to stay and promised to never do it again. A few months later we got orders to Taiwan, but briefly returned home to Cleveland, and got married on March 17th, St. Patrick's Day.

I will never forget that day. His sister and I went to pick up the cake and a few other things for the reception that evening. I remember so vividly my father saying to me, "I don't care if you're going down the aisle and change your mind at the last minute, it's ok!". We got married that evening and by the time people began to leave the reception, a freak snowstorm came out of nowhere, and cars had to literally be shoveled out of the driveway. It was crazy! The very next day we got into a heated argument over a guitar I had lent to a friend and were contemplating having the marriage annulled. My father sat down, had a talk with us and advised us to try to work things out so, we did. The time came for Lee to leave to check in at the base in Taiwan and get everything situated for me to join him.

The day finally came for me to leave. I had never been out of the country before, so I was a little nervous, but excited, nonetheless. During my flight I sat next to a really nice lady and we talked most of the way. She told me that her husband was stationed at the Air Force base in Taipei, Taiwan - the capital where we would be landing. When I landed, I expected to see my husband waiting for me, but he was not there. Unable to speak the language and being on the other side of the world alone and afraid, I asked the lady who I had sat next to, if she and her husband would wait with me until Lee got there, and they did. We waited quite a while before she suggested we go to the counter of the airline that we came in on and leave my name along with her address and phone number, so when he arrived, he would be able to call me. I am so glad that God sees and knows everything ahead of time; that day he had positioned my guardian angels. It so happened that she and her husband knew the language and were able to speak and interpret for me. They took me to their home, where I showered and had dinner with their family. Around 7:00 pm the phone rang; it was Lee. Her husband left to pick him up and brought him back to the house. After he ate, we all sat around and talked for a while. Since it was late, her husband suggested we stay there for the night, but Lee insisted on staying at a hotel because we needed to get up early the next morning to catch the train back to Kaohsiung, where he was stationed.

When we got settled in at the hotel, I asked him why he was not there to meet me at the airport. He unapologetically told me that he had gone out the night before, woke up late and missed the first train. It takes at least 4 to 5 hours from Kaohsiung to Taipai and he had to wait for the second train. We caught the train out the next morning and arrived in Kaohsiung later that afternoon. It was in Taiwan where the physically abuse began.

Some of the first people Lee introduced me to were his friends, Gene and Aubry. We would go to their house at least two to three times per week. They were a very nice couple, however one day, I overheard Aubrey telling Lee that whenever Gene got out of line with him, he would slap her. I could not believe it because they seemed to be so happy. During one of our visits with them, we all decided to take a taxi and go sightseeing downtown. On the way, for some reason, Lee began to tell me that he had taken a couple of Taiwanese women over to Gene and Aubrey's house before I arrived. He asked Gene to confirm what he was telling me, but instead, she turned around and told him, "There is no way I would ever get your wife on the other side of the world and hurt her like that". When she said that, I knew what he said was true. He started playfully nudging me on my arm and teasing me about it. I pushed his hand back the first time, but he did it again. The second time, out of anger, I took his hand and slung it back, but this time it hit him in the face. He was embarrassed and told the driver to stop the taxi. He proceeded to jump out the car, came over to my side, opened my door, and backhanded me in the face. We were in the middle of downtown, with everyone watching but I did not care; I got out of the car and began to fight back, until Aubrey jumped in between us. Lee then flagged down another cab, pushed me inside and we headed home. I was hurt, confused and cried all the way to the house. He had waited until he got me on the other side of the world, away from my family and with no one to turn to for help.

When we got inside the house he began to cry and say, "I'm sorry, I love you and it'll never happen again". All I could do was cry and say, "I just want to go home". He apologized repeatedly and tried to hold me, but I did not want him to touch me. Eventually I forgave him, and things were going ok, but I began to walk on eggshells most of the time. There was always the fear of it happening again and

46

it did! Abuse is progressive, and with each episode, it became a little worse each time. It was hard for me to understand how someone who said they loved me could also turn around and abuse me at the same time. When I asked him to explain it to me, all he said was, "I do it because I love you and want you to act right."

Being in the military, we moved around a lot, so after Taiwan our next stop was Florida. Between destinations we would always return home to spend time with our families, so we flew back to Cleveland and stayed a couple of weeks before driving to Florida. The day we got to Florida, we had to go on base to find out where we would be staying until we found our own place. The young man assisting us gave Lee directions and proceeded to compliment me on my hair. Lee did not say anything at that moment but, when we got back in the car, his attitude towards me had changed. Then there was the rejection and the silent treatment. I later came to understand that this is also a form of abuse. Silence speaks loudly; it affects you both mentally and emotionally and is as cruel as any other form of abuse. I sat up that night looking out the window and crying until the sun came up wondering why in the hell I did not have the strength to leave. Of course, Lee slept all night, got up the next morning, got dressed and left to process his paperwork on the base.

Over time, it appeared things were getting better. We became friends with several married couples whose relationships were great, and we seemed to fall right in line with them. A year later I became pregnant with our first daughter, Nikki, and I was sure this would bring about a permanent change in our relationship. (Remember, there can be long periods of time between abusive episodes, leading one to think that the abuser has changed). When I was about three months pregnant, he began to stay away from home for hours at a time and I noticed a change in his

47

attitude. One evening when he came home, I met him out front because I had a terrible headache and asked for the keys to the car to go to the emergency room. He thought I was having a miscarriage and said, "What I prayed for is finally happening." When I told him, I was not having a miscarriage he snatched the car keys away from me, and as I began to walk down the sidewalk back towards to the house, I could feel that something was about to happen. Suddenly, for no reason, he punched me in the back of my head. I quickly got inside the house and found something to grab to protect my baby and myself. I threatened to hit him if he came near me and eventually, he went and sat down in the living room. I wanted to leave and call my father, but I was sure Lee would not let me leave without a fight and the closest phone was at least five to seven minutes away. So early the next morning, I pretended to take our dog out for his morning walk, and I ran to the nearest phone booth and called my father. I told him what happened the night before and asked if he could send me money for a plane ticket home. He agreed to wire the money and told me to call him later to find out where I could pick it up. When I called back, my mother answered and told me that after I had spoken with my father that he came home, packed a bag, got in the car and was headed to Florida to get me. When he arrived late that night, he told me to go pack my things, sat down in the kitchen, all the while with Lee sitting in the living room. I felt safe. We left out that morning, heading back to Cleveland.

I was now back home, four months pregnant, safe but confused, not knowing what would become of my marriage. I did not talk to Lee my first few days home, but gradually we began talking on the phone nearly every day while I stayed home trying to sort things out. This continued for a few months, with him telling me how much he loved and missed me and so I eventually agreed to go back. Of course, when you return, everything seems to be great, but it was only a matter of time before his old ways resurfaced.

We welcomed our first daughter, Nikki, on April 2, 1975. I was so elated but what I thought would bring Lee and I closer together, did not really make much of a change. In fact, he became increasingly jealous of the time I spent taking care of her. When she was year old, she had severe case of diarrhea for several days and no matter what we gave it her, it did not help. So, we took her to the base hospital where they gave her medicine to help her keep food down, but it did not work. After this continued for three more days, I finally found the culprit. Apparently, the night we visited a friend's house to play cards, she had eaten a cigarette butt from their ashtray. I immediately asked Lee if he would take us to the hospital off base for her to be treated, but he refused. So, I carried my daughter, one block over, to a friend's house and she and her husband took us to the emergency room off base. I had endured his abuse over the past few years, but this was a completely different level for me. This was my baby, who could have possibly died, had I not asked my friend to take me off base to the hospital. I called my father and asked him to send me money to come home; in the meantime, the baby and I stayed over my friend's house until the money came through. The second day we were there, he came over and tried to take the baby from me, I held her tight, but he continued to pull her, so, to keep him from injuring her, I let go! Our friends were yelling at him and trying to talk some sense into to him - finally he gave her back to me and left.

When the money arrived, I got our tickets and flew home to Cleveland. I had missed my cycle for that month and found out shortly afterward, that I was now pregnant with my second child, Kenyada. I remained in Cleveland until after she was born. When she was about three months old, we returned, once again, to Florida to reunite with Lee. What was it that kept drawing me back to him? Why could I not break free? I know it may sound crazy to some of you and maybe you find yourself in the same position. Just know that there is hope and light at the end of the tunnel.

For almost a year, things were tolerable; there was no physical abuse, but there was a lot of jealousy and verbal abuse. One day, we attended one of the base picnics where they had drinks, bar-b-que, and games; it was fun, but when the liquor ran out Lee asked me to go down the street to the liquor store. When I got back, I handed him the bottle with his keys, and sat down to finish enjoying the rest of the time we had left. After everything was over, everybody began to pack up and leave. I got to the car with the girls before he did; he was still walking and talking with the guys. When he got to the car, he reached in his pocket for his keys, but, did not have them. He asked me if I had them and I told him no and reminded him that I had given them to him when I handed him the bottle of liquor. He basically called me a liar and hit me in the face (he always made sure to hit me there.) His friend, Sargent Brumfield, came over and told him to stop and suggested they go back to the table where we had been sitting to see if the keys were there and that is exactly where he found them. He got in the car and we all left.

To get to our house, we had to travel about two miles down a long dark road. He was so intoxicated that he was swerving off the road. I tried not to say anything, but, my babies were in the car, and I did not know if he was nodding off, so I lightly touched the side of the steering wheel to keep it on the road and told him that he was drifting off to the side a little. He started yelling and asking me why I had been looking across the park at some guy when we were at the picnic. He said, "don't you know that I love you?" I tried to assure him that it was not true, but he took the back of his hand and began to back hand me, one blow after another, to the side of my head. I was holding my youngest daughter Kenyada in my arms at the time and could not take it anymore, so I began to think of how I could jump out the car and toss her back on the seat. He saw me reaching for the handle of the door and started slowing the car down. I saw the headlights of another car behind us and I made up my mind that I was going to jump out and run to the other car for help, but when I got out, he stopped and ran over to where I was, put his arms around me, and made it seem like we were just standing on the side of the road hugging. He made me get back in the car. When we got to the house, I went into the bathroom to look at my face. The entire left side of my face was swollen and disfigured. The baby was crying, and so I walked into the kitchen to fix her a bottle, but he would not let me fix it. I told him to look at what he had done to my face. He told me that I better not move and if I did, he would make the other side of my face look the same way. After about fifteen minutes, he walked into the living room. I started fixing her bottle, while he was still saying all kinds of derogatory things to me.

At one point, he stood with his hands stretched out like he was Jesus hanging on the cross and saying, "Look at him! Look how they nailed Him to the cross!". His voice had changed, and he began speaking in a demonic tone. I refused to look. He told me to put my hand on the bible and swear that I was not looking at the guy across the park, but I refused. After hitting me again and knocking me across the room he threatened to put his fist through my face. He then sat down on the couch and began to play his guitar; while he was playing, he started nodding off and finally he went into a deep sleep. Just to make sure he was in a sound sleep, I began making loud noises to see if it would awaken him, but he was out cold. When I was sure, I left the girls in the bed and ran a block away to my friend's house, Inez. She and her husband had also attended the picnic that day

51

and were in bed asleep. I knocked on the door, but nobody answered. I ran around to her bedroom window, knocked on it, but still no answer. As I returned to the front door, she opened it. When she saw my face, she put her hand up to her mouth and started screaming. I told her that I did not have much time and asked her to please get dressed, come get the girls and I and take us out to Sargent Brumfield's house, which was about thirty minutes away. I told her, "I'm gonna run back to the house, grab some clothes and put them outside. Don't blow the horn or turn on the headlights; I'll be looking out the window and when I see you pull up, I'll bring the girls out, one at a time". It only took her about ten minutes, but it seemed like hours. I grabbed one of my daughters, ran and put her in the car, came back in, made sure he was still asleep, grabbed the other one, secured her in the car and headed to Sargent Brumfield's house.

When we got there, I asked he and his wife if we could please stay there because I knew he would never think to come out there. Inez went back home and called my mother to tell her what happened. She said, "I think the bones in her face are broken". I called the base police and they went to house and arrested him. The following day, I went to the hospital; thankfully nothing was broken. I returned the home next day, but we had very few words. The next morning, while I was watering the grass, I heard a car behind me and when I turned around it was my family; my father, mother and sister had driven all the way from Cleveland to pick me up. When my father saw what Lee had done to me, I saw a look on his face that I had never seen before. He then told me very plainly, "If Lee says so much as 'hello' to me, I will drop him", and I knew he would do exactly what he said. Lee was at work at the time and they were hungry, so we went to the store to get some food. We returned home and while my mother was preparing it, Lee walked in. I remembered my father's words, and for the first time, by the grace of God, Lee did not open his mouth. He just walked around the house but never said a word. After we finished eating, we rested until the next morning before leaving for Cleveland.

I stayed gone for three years. During that time, I got a job, the girls and I moved into our own place and I began dating again. We were happy. Lee would call my parents' house occasionally, but my and dad would tell my mom not to tell me, for fear that I would go back. One day while at my mother's house, the phone rang. My mother picked it up and told me that I had a phone call; I picked up the phone and it was Lee. He told me that he had been calling, but I was never there. We began talking again and he started telling me how he had given his life to the Lord, was in church and attending bible study at someone's house during the week and was a changed man. We talked almost every day; he would quote scriptures and talk about the bible and I bought into it again. When he got orders to Virginia, he told me that when he got ready to leave Florida, he was going to drive home, come and get me and the girls and take us with him. We went to Virginia and stayed for about 6 years with only one physical alteration, but many other challenges. I was working at the hospital at night and attending Nursing school in the morning. Things were going smoothly but a few months before taking my state exam, he received orders to Germany, and I dropped out of school.

We arrived in Germany in 1987 and welcomed our third daughter, Christine, three months later in May; after going back for my six-week check-up, I was told that I was pregnant, yet again. Our fourth daughter, Yolanda was born in August 1988. My first two daughters were getting older, and by now Lee was starting to pick at them by saying little hurtful things, but I would always go to their defense. He knew not to touch them, or he would see a side of me that should have come out a long time ago. He knew my girls were my heart and I would defend them at all costs. It is funny that I would not do that when it came to myself (remember I said earlier that abuse had stages of progression.) Three years had gone by and we returned to the states, with orders to Las Vegas. After being here close to a year, he began to drink heavily. I do not know if he started back on drugs or not, but the verbal abuse was taking its toll on me and the girls. We were miserable, and in one of our last arguments, he told me that he could kill me, bury my body in the desert and they would never find me. I knew then, that God was telling me that this was the last straw and we had to leave; I could feel God telling me, "let this be your exodus before somebody becomes a statistic." He did not know it, but, one day when he was at work I went and put a deposit down on an apartment for me and my kids, and when he got home, we were gone. I will never forget the feeling when we walked into that apartment - there was a sense of freedom and the peace and joy on my kids' faces was everything to me. I struggled for a while, but it was all worth it. My oldest daughter, Nikki and I both got jobs working construction and became electricians. God opened doors, answered prayers and showed up at every turn. In case you are wondering, sure, he tried to get with me, but there was no looking back. I was finally free and realized that I was worth more than that. God gave me renewed strength and enabled me to move forward with my life. I filed for divorce and no, Lee did not go without a fight; it took five years for it to be completed. When we went before the court and everything was finalized, reality set in that it was indeed over. I broke down and cried, and surprisingly Lee did too. The hell that I had lived through was no more. I was free.

So, you may be thinking, "What happened next?". The next stage of my life was that of forgiveness, but how do you forgive someone that caused you so much pain and took so much from you? Is that even possible? I am here to tell you, yes, it is. The greatest lesson I had to learn is that true freedom comes when you are able to forgive the one that wronged you and to also forgive yourself. When I learned that true forgiveness was not for him but for me, that is when God made it possible to be completely free, and forgiveness became my crown. And I wear it with pride.

I have since remarried, my children are now grown, flourishing and have families of their own. I am the proud grandmother of eighteen beautiful grandchildren, which I love dearly. I have shared my life experiences with them to let them know that they are valued and should never ignore red flags. We must teach people to know their worth. No one has the right to put their hands on anyone, no matter who it is, and if they need help leaving, we need to be able to show them the way out, before it is too late. If what I went through was to help someone else, it was all worth it. I have learned along this journey that I am valuable and the only thing people can do to you is what you allow; when you know your worth, you will not settle for less.

I chose to be free from bitterness!
I chose to be free from pain and hatred!
I chose to be open for God's love and blessings!
I choose to FORGIVE

FORGIVENESS BECAME MY CROWN!

Andrea Dixon Reed

Andrea Dixon Reed is a Brooklyn, New York born native, raised in Greensboro, N.C. She is a graduate of Carolina School of Broadcasting in Charlotte, N.C. Andrea defines being a wife and mother her most successful accomplishments. She is a motivational speaker, relationship coach, actress, travel agent and now co-author. She has served in several stage plays, TV/radio edit bits and is the visionary of an informative relationship panel called "Fire and Desire" that speaks on today's issues in "Marriage and Monogamy", "Dating to Marry", "Single and Satisfied", "Divorce" and "Blended families". Her love and belief in Christ allow her continuous pursuit of happiness.

Her mission is to do the things in life that brings joy and remain passionate about it! Andrea is a survivor of sexual, physical and emotional abuse. The objective and focus of her writing is to share her story around the nation and to empower others to overcome a victimized mindset.

First, I want to dedicate this writing to my Lord and Savior Jesus Christ; without Him nothing is possible. Thank you for allowing your grace to become surreal and sufficient in my life - I am your "Sozo" favorite daughter!

To my Husband Linell A. Reed, my protector, strength, rock, and provider who has helped me transition into the butterfly that God has destined me to become: Thank you for loving my "crazy", sexy and cool, (LOL) and sticking with me through thick and thin. Thank you, dear husband, for allowing me the gifts of loving my bonus children Sanya and Zamaria Reed.

To my most precious possessions, my children Dajha M. Huggins, Deshawn M. Huggins and Donovan P. Huggins, who have witnessed the distress and pain that mommy's been through, but have always stuck by my side and loved me without judgment, I love you with all my heart, forever and always!

To my parents Sherry/James Phelps and Melvin S. Dixon, thank you for loving me without conditions. Thank you for teaching me who I am and to never to settle for anything less than God's best. I may not have always applied those principles in my youth, but the woman I am today is all because of what was instilled in me and I am forever grateful.

To my grandmother Violet Carson, grandmother Bernella Rowe, and great grandmother Mildred Carson, may you forever rest in peace, I pray that I have made you proud.

To my Pastors Lee and Shonia Stokes of Destiny Christian Center in, Greensboro, N.C.: Thank you for the accepting the call on your lives to pastor and teach your flock the true Word of God! I never would have never learned and understood the loving Grace of God and His unconditional love for me without your teaching.

To Pastor Brandi Rojas, thank you for the opportunity to become a co-author and share my story with the world for God's Glory.

To my mother-in- love Ms. Beverly B. Nole, I appreciate your continuous support, wisdom and love.

To all my siblings, family, extended family, and friends, I love you with all my heart and truly appreciate your impact and support in my life.

Connect with Andrea

Email: andreadreed@yahoo.com

CHAPTER 4

Soteria Girl

Webster Dictionary describes rage as "violent, uncontrollable anger." (Merriam-Webster's Collegiate Dictionary, 1999). Rage can and will destroy a person's life if it is not dealt with and can ultimately become deadly to you or someone else. Many who suffer from this uncanny disorder typically have a "why", behind it. We hear of stories daily in the media of different acts of rage, whether it be road rage incidents, physical assaults in relationships or involving people who may not even know each other but are at the wrong place at the wrong time. The scenarios mentioned above are all associated with RAGE characteristics. The question that I must ask the masses is this: How did it all begin? What are the triggers? What, if anything, can be done about it? I cannot find an answer for the many who deal with this disorder, but I can identify how it showed up in my life and the triggers associated with it.

Understanding how rage transpired in my life also allowed me to understand "*God's Grace*", in my life. I started asking myself "after all that I have been through and allowed myself to go through, what process did I need to learn?", and the questions that are even more important, "How will I positively share and help someone else through this process? Will I be able to identify with those people by sharing my truth or would I be judged?" God's answer to me was simple," both will occur" but when doing God's will it is beneficial physically, emotionally, spiritually and financially. We are all taught not to question the reason why life happens the way it does whether good, indifferent or what we consider as bad, but can we be honest enough to say that we have all contemplated it anyway? Have you ever looked at someone else that just seemed to have what we considered to be the "perfect life", not knowing what all they had to sacrifice to get there? God's way came with a price, and the price was Jesus who paid it all with His shed blood on the cross for you and me. As I begin to share my story, keep in mind that I am aware of who I am today and whose I am! I have not always been this person, but I now know why I went through some battles and chose the wrong paths at times. I now know that even through the "fire", God was still there. Even though I had to sweat a little, His perfect *"Grace"* kept me so that I would not perish. I certainly weathered the storm of mass destruction, and for those that feel they that may have no voice or may have allowed their current circumstance to outweigh them, then please continue to read. Unfortunately, there are people who I loved and were close to that I wish could have read this content but have since passed away. I had friends that felt their mishaps, or mistakes were bigger than Gods love for them and have ended their lives, because of *mere* mental torment. Their tragedies left me with the question: what if there was more that I could have said or done to stop them from pursuing death? If I only knew at that time the real love of God and how much compassion and love He has for us all, then maybe I could have made a difference and changed the mindsets of those who walked in pure reproach. I may not have been able to make a big difference in the lives of those who have passed, but I feel that my calling is to continue to shed light on His perfect love for us and as long as I have breath in my body, I will forever always thank God for what He has done for me, and what He continues to do!

SOTERIA GIRL!

I was the typical young girl growing up. I played with dolls, played sports, had friends, was blessed with a very loving family and wanted for absolutely nothing. I had life's necessities and if I desired anything else, I got that too. I was raised in the church and was always taught that if I kept God first and obeyed my parents, life would line up. My perception of God at that time was that you did not break "rules", because if you did, you were going to hell! As a child that's "scary as hell". Me being young, immature and having no "relationship" with God, I viewed Him as terrifying (being afraid creates a cynical relationship). I specified no *relationship* because there is a huge difference between religion and relationship!

My mom, dad and I still resided in Brooklyn, New York. My father was a hard-working man, who worked long hours to provide for his family because it was in his culture; he was a Jamaican-born native that believed in success at all cost. My mother was a banker who did what it took to make sure her daughter was taken care of. I remember visiting family in the Carolinas as a child. I also remember my mother discussing our transition from New York to North Carolina one day. She thought it would be better for me growing up there. I felt different about her decision because there was something that I was withholding from her. Being a youth, I did not feel comfortable conversing on certain matters and honestly did not have a clue on how to feel.

I remember her talking to me about sex and appropriate versus inappropriate touching and if someone ever touched me inappropriately to always tell her or my father. Now thinking back, what was an inappropriate touch? How would you know if it was inappropriate at such a young age? What if a person that you are supposed to trust touches you in that manner? These are some of the questions that most children have. My mother told me where no one should ever touch me, but being a child, I was confused in my little six-year-old mind. I did not fully comprehend what was going or what even to believe or do about it. "Despite the warnings, molestation showed up and soon became a reality in my young life. I was constantly around this person because it was a family member; I was around him so much that I started believing his touches were all love or at least this was what he made me to believe.

63

My mind was manipulated into thinking that this was a good thing and that I should appreciate it. The touches occurred quite often when we would visit North Carolina. The things that were taking place started to feel "normal" and eventually progressed from touches to sexual acts. I remember the person telling me to be quiet and to never tell what was taking place. He never opposed a threat but made it known that he "loved me". This went on from the early age of six years old on up until eleven or twelve.

By this time, I became a very good performer. By this I mean "act" as if you are normal, everything will be fine and that what I am enduring (memory, feelings) would eventually go away, right? Going into my teenage years, I started developing and experiencing different emotions and feelings as most teens do. The difference for me was identifying with who I was as an adolescent and secretly coping with the molestation that I went through. I disliked myself and what I saw in the mirror. All I could see was an image of disgust and the belief that the things that happened to me was all my fault. The devil condemned me for something I had no control over, and I bought into his lie. This was the moment when **RAGE** started to define me. By this time my mom and dad split up and we moved to North Carolina; as to be expected, the distance caused us to live separate lives. My father stayed in New York because of his business. He would come to visit us often, and we traveled to visit family as well. This was around that time in my life that I started dating even though I knew that I was not ready; being molested changed me from the young lady that I was supposed to become, to a person I grew to dislike. I started thinking boys were my answer to solve my pain and depended on them for my happiness. HUGE MISTAKE!!!

My first boyfriend was a player. He cheated like crazy and knowing what I know now, of course he did, we were teens and had no business dating! I unfortunately took so called "love" serious! The thought that someone would purposely hurt me left me in a place of indescribable pain. It got to the point that I became abusive - I would slap him for looking at other girls or talking to them. I fussed, cussed, fought him for cheating and then took him back when he apologized. (I now became the abuser!) My rage began to set in at an uncontrollable pace. I would accept whatever "life" threw at me. Bad relationships, temporary friends and unauthorized opinions. I allowed "man" to mold me into what he thought I should be. I made bad decisions because condemnation ruled my life for something that I had no control over. That abuse happened to me, and as a result, I victimized my internal thoughts. **Dating young can ruin your life and the lives of others!** My mother trusted me to make the right decisions because I led her to believe that she was able to do so. She had no clue of the things I had endured. My mom thought I was still a virgin, but in all actuality, that was stolen from me as a child. I knew how to be everything anyone wanted me to be; I wore a mask and learned at the tender age of thirteen how to be the "great pretender", just like my molester. My spiraling out of control never affected my grades surprisingly; matter of fact I managed to keep that part of my life together. I would rebel by coming home late after hanging with friends or not calling my mother out of *mere* courtesy to let her know I was ok or running late; that was me acting out when all I had to do was make the right decision by calling her. I constantly ended up on punishment and upset my mother over the smallest situations because of my bad decision making.

I never considered myself to be the popular girl in high school. I was not known as one of the "pretty" girls that I am aware of or the smartest, but after the tom boy phase left, I developed what was considered *"sex appeal"*. I had this *"strut"* and could give you a *"smile"* that melted any boy's heart. And I knew how to use my charm. I snuck and watched a lot of 90's movies that I had no business watching. Some of my favorites was *"Boomerang"*, *Dirty Dancing* and *Fatal Attraction*. Being young and impressionable and not knowing who I was, I started to take on the identities of certain characters portrayed in the movies. I started attracting the wrong attention by mentally "living in TV land". I started meeting different guy friends here and there, but it was not until the age of fifteen when I met the devil himself, Mr. D. He was from High Point N.C., and we met while I was working at Taco Bell as a teen. We never really considered ourselves an item; we were supposed to be like family. He was a bit older than I was, so at first, I looked at him like a brother. He would come to family functions and he had other girls that he dated, so at times he would introduce me to one or two of them. We hung together like homies. I would go to his house and his friends' homes. There was a slight crush but nothing that ever got serious, or even physical until one night we were on our way to a cookout.

Mr. "D" came and picked me up from my home where I lived with my mother, little brothers and dad (mom remarried, and he became like a father to me). Mr. "D" had his homeboy in the car who I knew well so I sat in the back seat and we took off. Nothing about that night was unusual - we listened to music, laughed and kicked it as always. The cookout was in High Point, so I was not familiar with the area, but I can recall him turning down this back road full high grass and gravel. I was comfortable with them, so I never expected what happened next. I remember the car coming to a stop. I just figured that they had gotten lost and was turning around. I asked them, "Where are we? Are we lost or something?" Mr. D looked at me in the rear-view mirror and said, "We are where we are supposed to be." He then turned up the music and then they opened the car doors. I started to panic because I knew something bad was about to take place; all I could think of was "not again!" The friend of Mr. D grabbed me by my arm and started to pull me out of the backseat. I screamed, kicked and

66

attempted to fight them off but absolutely nothing could stop the strength they had. All I could think was "They are going to kill me and leave my body right in these tall bushels!" His friend held my thin arms down while Mr. D pulled my jeans off and sexually assaulted me. He held his hand over my mouth as I cried tears of fear! It seemed as if he had enough stamina for hours, when in fact, the rape was over in a matter of minutes. I can recall laying there feeling nasty, disgusted and condemned once again. All I could do was think that this too was somehow my fault. Maybe it was the "strut" that led him to do this or a look of seduction I possibly gave him? I totally had to be at fault! Why else would my friend do this to me? After he raped me, he told me that this was how he proved he loved me, and that if I told someone about what happened he would hurt me. He did not fail to mention that he knew my family and where we lived and would cause harm to them. He told me to get myself together and that it was my fault that I made him feel this way about me. Mr. D then wiped my face and asked me If I was ready to eat as if this was a normal act for him. I looked at him with tears streaming down my face and humbly shook my head, yes. He wiped my tears and kissed me on the forehead. In my private thoughts I said to myself, "you see, I knew I was to blame, after all, I should not have made him feel this way."

On the way to the cookout, I told myself everything would be fine and that he only did this because I was so desirable and that he loved me. Over and over I rehearsed in my mind what I could have done differently so this would never happen again. On the way back home, I immediately got into "character" and acted as if nothing ever happened. Mr. D got out the car and walked me up to the door, (portraying that protector role); my mom met us at the door and he even had the audacity to say to my mother, "hey *mom.*" My mother asked if we had a good time and he responded "*yes, a great time*", as if nothing ever happened, while I remained "in character" standing there smiling and agreeing with him but feeling like a used-up piece of trash. Shortly after that he told me he would page me later, gave me a hi-five and left. As I went upstairs, all kind of emotions ran through my head: fear, pain, anger, defeat! What should I do now? What if he gave me an STD? How would I explain that? I took my shower and silently cried the entire night. The next day I kept pondering on whether I should be honest with my family, and let them know the real deal, but all I kept pondering is what would happen to them if I told. What if he and his friends came back and killed my family and I? My homegirl called me the next day to see how the cookout went and as I planned, I led her to believe that Mr. D and I had consensual sex for the first time, and how wonderful it was. I told her how much he said he loved me and desired me all the while knowing what the truth was — knowing that I did not ask for this, but I guess I deserved it.

Occasionally, the rapist would page me and call the house phone every so often, not to check on me but to ensure our secret was still a secret. He would plant lies in my head saying that he loved and missed me, how pretty I was, and the list went on. I did not see him for a long time after he raped me. A couple of months went by and I noticed that I had symptoms of nausea and a lot of saliva build up in my mouth. I would wake up in the morning feeling sluggish and horrible; not understanding it all I told my friend about the experience I was going through. My friend advised me that I was possibly pregnant, and I would need to get a test done. I took a pregnancy test and my worst fear came true; it was positive. I was scared out of my mind and could not believe that this was happening to me! I knew nothing about babies and pregnancy not to mention that I was only sixteen years of age. I was trying my best to hide my morning sickness and sleepiness. The symptoms I had was obvious of pregnancy, but I could not allow my parents to notice it. I did not want them to find this out knowing the hurt and disappointment it would cause. As days and weeks went by, I needed to know how to handle this. My friend told me to talk to my mother but neither one of them knew the truth of how I got pregnant not to mention, all I could think about was that my mom trusted me and surely this would hurt her! Like I said, she believed that I was a virgin and that I had never encountered sex.

As time passed my stomach got bigger. I tried wearing big shirts to camouflage the fact but that did not work. My friend asked what I was going to do. I begged my friend not to tell her, but she knew she had to; a decision needed to be made on whether or not I was going to keep it and time was ticking. I ended up having an abortion. I felt I had no choice; I did not want a baby, and especially one under this set of circumstances. Condemnation was destroying me - I was hurt from having an abortion, did not know how to tell my mom the truth about my pregnancy and had insurmountable guilt for breaking my mother's trust and heart. I was not out here being promiscuous, but she did not know that. No one knew the truth but God, me, the rapist and his friend. Years went by and I my patterns worsened; I seemed to attract all of the wrong guys in my life.

I finished high school and went to college at G.T.C.C. where I met Mr. T. He was beautiful to the eye, seemed highly intelligent, shy but engaging and appeared to be completely in "awe" about me. We started dating and he had this way of making me feel like I was the only girl in the room. At the time, he gave me what I assumed I needed, affirmation. We were both in school aspiring to be something in life. This new love seemed to innocent and right. I was young and foolish at eighteen years of age. I pretended that all was together on my end and that I was ready to date! I was working various jobs, in school, and was getting my life together by aspiring to do something to make my family proud. Mr. T appeared to be perfect and because I did not put two and two together, I thought he was highly protective over me and had my back. The truth was it became obsession (to my young readers, this is a sure sign of control). He did not want me out of his sight. He had to have all my time and attention and got jealous if I chose to hang with friends and even family. When he came around my family, he was never social, but instead kept his head down as if he was hiding something. It was so embarrassing. I would think to myself, "Talk or say something, man!" My mother told me something about this guy was all the way off; my mother's intuition was always right about family and friends! She kept on telling me that he acted extremely possessive and that one day he would hurt me. I ignored all the signs, but they were obvious. I attempted to sign up for flight attendant training and he signed up too. I took an interest in real estate and he came along too. Everything I aspired to pursue, he tried doing the same thing. He would apply where I worked and that became weird. I asked him "What are your goals in life?", and he said, "whatever yours are." I should have run for the hills but instead, my battered mind told me *this was real love.*

I remember meeting him at the mall on a Saturday afternoon. He immediately grabbed me, hugged me and said that he missed me, although we had just seen each other the night before. We were in the mall for maybe an hour before some guy from school greeted me and asked how I was doing. I introduced the boyfriend to my friend from school, but his entire demeanor changed; I had never seen him act like this! He immediately grabbed me up by my arm and demanded, "I'm ready to go!" As we started walking abruptly through the mall, I jerked my arm from him and asked him what the hell was wrong with him. He looked at me as if he could kill me and **punched me dead in my face**. I fell backwards in dismay, but mostly ashamed because of the people that witnessed it. I ran after him like a fool wanting to know why "he was mad." He yelled out "*you want to be with that boy.*" The longer I stayed with him the worse the abuse got; he beat me like crazy! After the

70

assault he would just apologize and cry as if my scarred face or body hurt him so!

Later, Mr. T applied for a job at the same place I worked for. I was a team lead in a call center and, with no help from me, he got the position. One day, he saw me training one of the new guys in my department and got pissed off. After work he asked me if I could drive him home; he had a car, so I was unsure why he needed me to, but I did anyway. For the first three to five minutes he was silent. I automatically knew that indicated an issue and braced myself for what would happen next. When I asked him if something was wrong, he started getting upset saying the guy that I trained had a crush on me and we were flirting with one another. I advised him of how pathetic he sounded, and the guy and I had nothing but a work relationship. While I was driving, he punched me in my head, causing the car to start swerving; I tried my best to control the steering wheel and attempt to block the punches all at the same time. This crazed man somehow grabbed my pointer finger and bended it all the way back until it popped. He broke my finger and the pain was excruciating. It swelled up like a water balloon. I went through absolute hell with this man. He would bite plugs of skin off me leaving bruises and bite marks all over my body. I remember him beating me up and taking the keys to my vehicle. I attempted to get them back through the driver's window while he was in driver's seat; he rolled up the windows while my arms were still inside the car and drove off as I ran with the car. I eventually got tired to the point that my legs started dangling and got skinned up as he continued to drive. At one point I ended up pregnant with his baby and while fighting he kicked me in the stomach; this impact caused me to lose our child. Another incident took place: one night we were at the movies and I told him I had to leave to get back home. He beat me and left me unconscious in a ditch to die. It got to the point that I knew a butt whooping was coming every day. My esteem

71

was so shot he started telling me how I was not his type and did not look like his ex-girlfriends. He told me that he liked to beat me because I was not a white woman and that he did not respect me as a black woman. I said well "If you want a white woman, please go and find one", but he told me that he liked to see me suffer.

He became Ike and I was Tina, but I started to fight back. I had so much resentment in me from years of abuse that I became a ticking time bomb. If someone challenged me or did something that I felt was disrespectful, we would fight; I became fearless. All of this built-in anger and rage from one toxic relationship to the next became a caution for those around me. My patterns of life continued with meaningless relationships and I carried baggage from years of pain. I dated drug dealers, athletes, businessman, but I still could not find what I was looking for. I never started fights, but when it got the point where someone wanted to start a beef with my friends, I was the person that would fight on their behalf. The rage took over me in the blink of an eye. If someone blew their horn at me at a stop light, they should have also prepared ahead of time to have a bad day because I was coming for them. If someone mumbled something under their breath, smart comments or anything, you could just about guarantee that they were going to end up getting cut, beat up and so forth. That rage became my persona and it was horrible. When I let loose, everything that was done to me would come up in that moment. I wanted love and acceptance and in that stage of my life no man could offer me that. You can never fill a void where God is supposed to be. I was looking for love in all the wrong places when the entire time God was trying to fill the voids of my hurt and pain!

I had my daughter in 2001. One month before I had her, I sat my mother down to finally tell her about the molestation and rape. All my mother could do was cry, especially when I told her who I was molested by. Keeping

72

these secrets ruined my childhood and a lot of my adult life. It explained why I was so rebellious and promiscuous and started looking for acceptance in man all because I rejected myself. My mom asked what happened to my rapist and where he was; years later I learned that he was imprisoned for molestation and raping girls and throughout the years his rap sheet grew. No, he did not stop at me - he went to the next, then then next and so forth. If there is someone reading my story and it resonates with you or you have been through this and have not told anyone, please, I beg you to do so - you can save yourself a lifetime of pain and bad choices.

You see, God was speaking through me with all the obstacles that I went through. Relationship with Him was key to it all; accepting His Grace was way more love than I could had ever received from man. My life was a picture of **Soteria/Sozo,** and of course I did not know that at the time. **Soteria** in the Greek means "deliverance, preservation, safety and salvation." **Sozo** in Hebrew means "saved, whole, healed or preserve." When I learned to understand the meaning, it spoke volumes to me. I had been through a series of trauma, heart breaks and upsets only to cover it up with excuses and try to be an overachiever with success! One thing for sure, the truth always comes out; you cannot hide or fight those demons alone. I took my family through hurt and pain. I would not be able to explain it all in this writing because my story is a lifetime of truths. What I want you to understand is God's unconditional love for you. We cannot separate ourselves from Him; His love is the unconditional, underserved, unearned favor of God.

When I learned this key principle my *relationship* with my Savior begin. My Pastor, Lee Stokes started teaching on the Grace of God around 2008; in this series, we were taught what the true love of God meant. You see, it was not about me this entire time but instead, all about Jesus' finished work on the cross. I kept my focus on the wrong situations for so long and doing so only allowed me to make decisions that continued to hurt me. After having my children, I realized God trusted me to raise them, so why not raise them in grace? I often think about all the years that I wasted on "situation-ships" when God was there with His arms extended for me the entire time. God is not a man that He shall lie, so if we desire love and wealth, He will honor those things, but we must learn to go to Him and ask Him to provide us with what we desire. He will give it to us in His timing and not our own. If you ask me if I still battle with rage, my answer is: though at times I can still get heated I never allow it to go to the extreme. I have a way to channel it now because I first asked God to renew my mind and heart. This does not happen overnight.

Forming true relationship with Him and understanding that if He is for me, why "fret" over those against me is the truth that I had to embrace. I am a lot more mature than I was years ago; my thought process is different, and I always avoid conflict and protect my peace. Is this easy? Yes and No. Choose different environments. Change the old company you keep and make sure that those around you have just as much self-control and respect the change in you; do not allow "just anyone" to come into your life. Know you are worth more than price tags.

One thing I know for sure: living a life of rage is not worth getting arrested or killed over and it is not worth hurting anyone over either. When I encounter a negative situation, I immediately render my thoughts and ask Jesus for help. I know my limit and I know what can take me over the edge and refuse to give the enemy power. Therapy is another way of taking control over the situation; it is called being accountable and mature. Some individuals do not believe in therapy - I used to be one of them but that is where I was seriously mistaken. If you do not feel that seeking counsel will help you, you are doing yourself a huge injustice. For me, I need Godly wisdom so I would rather go to someone who has spiritual nourishment and can give me biblical insight; whether it is church, someone outside of church such as a women's resource group, school counselors, help groups, or advocates for women's rights, find someone you can trust and start your healing process. Had I done this earlier, I could have saved myself years of pain, bad mistakes and ceased hurting others. I believe in all of you who have been through hurtful events like me. I pray the little that I shared reaches every person that needs this. Remember, to keep God first and everything else will be added to you, and always guard your heart.

I am happily married today to a man that loves me without conditions. He puts me right after God and would part the Red Sea for me if he could. I never thought I would ever see this day. We share everything together, without shame or embarrassment. He loves my children as if they were biologically his own and I am forever thankful. Just think, if I would have settled for abuse, pain, condemnation and shame, where would I be? I would have never had all that God has blessed me with or been able to accept true love. God will give you the desires of your heart. Keep Him first in all things, whatever you cannot endure, He has a perfect will for your life.

The Princess of Poetry,

Janelle Strickland

The Princess of Poetry, Elder Janelle Strickland, is a native of North Carolina. Born an only child "Princess" began writing at age eight. Princess is the proud mother of four children and two grandchildren. She attends Maximizing Life Family Worship Center and serves as Elder, Chief of Staff, Lead Armor Bearer and Project 5:2 Thanksgiving Coordinator under Pastors Omar and Brandi Rojas. She has birthed a prophetic, healing and deliverance ministry as a result of her dedication to God.

She is a nationally, multi award winning, professional spoken word artist, radio host, and entrepreneur of: The Princess of Poetry Entertainment Group, The HEART for Lupus Foundation, Strickland Design Group, Princess Designs-and The Princess Travels. She uses each day to live out her purpose and give the gift of hope.

May my story inspire & bless you? The Princess of Poetry

The Princess of Poetry, Janelle Strickland's Dedication

To God: first for helping me to survive with victory, over the many obstacles contained and outlined herein.

To my four children, Mia, Jay, Pat and Von. In addition, I dedicate this to my grandchildren, Leo and Neya: May my story bless your life for years and generations to come.

To everyone who has ever been rejected, to every person suffering from lupus, congestive heart failure, cancer and chronic illness warrior who is battling a diagnosis, facing obstacles in life or simply those who are looking to defeat any and everything the enemy is sending your way: Your story has purpose. Your voice carries strength and power. Someone out there needs to hear your story! Tell it; scream it if you have to.

Daily motto:
MAKE EVERY BREATH COUNT FOR SOMETHING GREAT!

Connect with TPOP

Phone: (336) 517-7255

www.facebook.com/DesignsByTPOP

Email: princessdesignsflowers@gmail.com

CHAPTER 5

In Between The Lines

One of the most painful rejections to get over is that of your parents. Let me explain.
This story of rejection starts off with a poem.

I sat down on the edge of rejection and pain.
Contemplating my escape, I vowed never to be found again
in this place again.
My destination tours were my mom and dad.
They quit before I could come out leaving me lost, broken
and sad.
I was not meant to ever be brought into this emotional corn
maze!
I was born out of love, not created as the evidence of their
failure and mistakes.
I was the first living adult abortion,
Follow me through and you will see exactly what I mean by
this notion
I was snatched from my safe place; naked and surrounded
in a pool of blood, they disassembled me limb from limb
with their sterile tools of hate.
By the time I even realized I wanted to live, it was almost
too late.

DAMAGE DONE!!

Now they view me as a reminder of the hurt they caused
each other and like their issues, they would prefer not to
deal with me.
I was a constant reminder of what should have been but
never would be.
Their inability to resolve their own guilt and pain would
become my daily torture, torment and truth.
My mother's drug addiction and my father's depression
killed every part of my youth.

My outdoor playtime was filled with creating ways to
escape the iron fist of abuse.
I'd jump up and down, waving arms at airplanes hoping
and praying for a rescue.

They all dwelled in silence hearing my screams amid her
cussing and tongue- lashing intimidation.
No one ever came. Not even after the bruises told their
story linking her to my incarceration.
Although, this sentence seemed to be for life my desire to
escape never left me
I realized my parents could not assist in my freedom
because they were in the cells next to me.

The Mother

She was born in a small city and was the only child
of her parents. Her relationship with her father was strong.
Her relationship with her mother was built on constant
abuse. Her mother had managed to raise her with an iron
fist, wicked mouth and negativity. Mother lived up to every
misguided and hateful word curse her mother ever uttered.
She became the reality of her mother's words after years of
trying to please her unsuccessfully.

She married a minister and produced a seed that
would be raised on her drug abuse and his absence and
depression. The marriage would not last but the wounds this
break up caused would never heal. She would walk under
the curse the rest of her life self-medicating with street
drugs to force her into the only euphoric pseudo happiness
she could find. She wanted a release from the pain of
living and that escape could only be found in the artificial
self-induced occurrences that only her drug abuse could
create.   Her daughter would be an audience of one
that had a VIP seat to view all that played out in her life.

80

This vantage point would shape her daughter into something she would later not even recognize. She continued to suffer from unmentionable pain - as in she never explained her pain and never got over it. Suffering in her own silence she chose to never give her pain a voice. Eventually, she would not even acknowledge the seed that she gave birth to. She exchanged the mother daughter relationship for something that she loved far greater.

Her mother was abusive. Her father left her mother because of the bitterness, constant anger, verbal abuse, physical abuse and ultimate unhappiness. He moved up north to New York and left his daughter, to suffer at the hand of her mother. This battle was one she could not win. Living with her mother was a terminal toxic environment. She became accustomed to the abuse and control of her own mother. This manifested as a duplication between her and her own daughter. She did not know how to love and show love; her mother never gave her that and was mean and hateful almost up to the moment she died. Her granddaughter would lead her mother to Christ a few months before her death. Only God knows if at the point of her transition, she was still professing Christ as her personal Savior. The seed she was used to try and kill, was the seed that ended up witnessing to her and birthing her soul salvation.

Once the mother was gone, she was alone in life; although the abuse had ended in the death of her mom, it continued to be a prisoner in the jail her mother built for her. The door was unlocked and open, but she had no idea how to live free outside of the prison she had made her home. She covered the bars with beautiful tapestries and delicately furnished it with care; she kept it spotless. It looked as if a professional designer created home sweet home there. No matter how lavish the furnishings, no matter how costly the furniture, a prison is still a prison. The prison was her safe place. Her prison became the site for her daughter's nervous breakdown.

The Father

He was raised in a two-parent family. His childhood was drastically different than that of Mother. His father was well known in the small town that he was raised in. His mother was also well known for her continuous love and support of her husband, the Pastor and Entrepreneur, as First Lady. Together they were pillars of the community and the glue that held the family together. He was the product of the wisdom and mantle of his great grandfather and his father. He would go on to be the third generation of ministers. His great grandfather was used to work miracles, signs and wonders and his father would go on to do the same. He had to carry the weight of the mantle and assignment of ministry but was not prepared for the temptations that would accompany it.

He married and the life of ministry began. He tried to duplicate what he had seen in his father from being by his side as he worked in the kingdom. He saw the long nights and days that his father put in because of the work of the Lord. He was in the services. He was a miracle. He had almost died when he was in high school and God performed a miracle that saved his life. He had the evidence of the word of God in his life. He was the living evidence that the prayers of the righteous availed much. He was on his death bed and God raised him up based on the prayers of his parents. There was no slighting the hand of God upon his life. Yet his ability to stay faithful to God became soiled in the transgressions he laid with.

His love for other women would be the demise of his marriage; that place would remain broken until the writing of this book. Failure of his marriage took him to a place of deep dark depression and hoarding. His life became about pretending to be something he was not. In an attempt to help him to increase the momentum of his ministry and continue to serve he was appointed as Pastor. This became another failure. He was eventually removed as Pastor for unethical handling of the church finances. He had remarried a woman who only pursued him as part of a bet to see who could get the preacher on their job. He fell for it. She was not quite first lady material. She and his daughter did not get along at all. His wife was almost the same age as his sister. Significantly younger, wilder and raised differently, she was not interested in being first lady nor having another child as a part of their union. Her son who was being raised by her mother and father was the only child she was willing to support or acknowledge. The abuse of his daughter continued for years as he watched. His daughter would blame him for years for the things he allowed his wife to do to his daughter.

At 16, his daughter was pregnant by her 22-year-old boyfriend. His wife took her to the doctor and confirmed the pregnancy. At the doctor appointment the stepmother informed his daughter that she would not be able to have the baby. She explained that the baby would not survive the pregnancy and she had to have an abortion. She told his daughter that this pregnancy would be too much for her and would possibly end her life as well. The daughter complied and went through the abortion. Later when the counselor came to visit his daughter at school and talk with her about the abortion to make sure she was in a good place mentally, the counselor asked if she was ok with her decision to end the pregnancy by ending the life of the child she was carrying. His daughter responded, "I had no choice. The baby was not fit to live and trying to have it could have killed me." The counselor looked confused and began to ask questions. She wanted to know who told her that. His daughter shared that her stepmother had told her. The counselor informed his daughter that this was not true. She turned to her aunt who helped her discover the truths behind what really happened. Hs wife had been sleeping with his daughter's boyfriend and cheating on her dad with other men. Rather than have another failed marriage, he sat and let his wife do whatever she wanted. He got tired of the constant fussing and fighting so he retreated into the comfort of his own demons. Depression kept him company. After a while of this, she opted to leave him, but they never divorced.

By this time, he had rejected his daughter and alienated her out of his life. He moved on to date another woman, moved in with her and took her children as his own. He had a new family. He had a new daughter that he proudly displayed and shared about. He never imparted into his own flesh and blood except for absence, no communication and depression. Eventually, he would not even talk to the one seed he birthed. He would reject her and replace the pain of the failed marriage to her mother with a whole new family in hopes of burying it. Eventually this relationship would dissolve as well. They were not married but to him, the hit felt the same. This would drive him so far into depression and isolation he became sick. Diagnosed with Cushing's disease, he would stop taking his life sustaining medication and be admitted to the hospital and his daughter would have to take over his care; she would have to go to his previous residence and collect all his belongings. His daughter took him in even though he was a stranger to her. Being the good child, she helped him get on his feet. She assisted him in getting his retirement payments and social security - she even got a larger apartment to accommodate him living with her until one day shortly after moving. She came home and he and all his belongings were gone. He had agreed to help with the rent. Now without his help, she would be evicted. She lost her home because of her sacrifices to help the father she really did not know who once again walked away from her. His rejection of her was right in line with that of her mother.

The Mother and Father

She was the evidence and constant reminder of their failure relationship - the evidence neither of them wanted to see or deal with. They fought over her in a custody battle all because of child support. Although infidelity was a common action on his part of the marriage, her father even went so far as to deny she was his because of her dark skin. Her mother had begun to see a dark-skinned Jamaican and he convinced his family, she cheated on him and I was not his child. Tests later would reveal this not to be true. At the time, it caused his daughter to be rejected, mishandled, mistreated and discriminated against by his family all because of the color of her skin (this was despite the fact; her mother and her mother's parents were very dark skinned.) The tug of war ended but the bruises left behind, never healed. They rejected their child. They left her to fight for herself. She was in the home of her mother but had no mother. Her father was in the same town and she never saw him or heard from him. She became the black sheep all because of the reputation of her parents. They left this child to be physically abused by her grandmother and/or in the home of her drug abusing mother.

This lifestyle, was not the ideal place for a child to grow up in. What she saw and experience in the drug parties, sex for drugs, people coming by to get high, selling drugs, and the person she became as a result of the pills, cocaine, weed and alcohol caused her to walk away from her child. Sometimes people in this position, think the child is better off if they are not in their life. You have got to read in between the lines; their pain caused her pain. Their pain caused them to reject their only child. She had to live under that rejection for years.

The Grand Mother

She was the meanest person you ever met. This was no joke. She managed to survive this way. Bitterness was her constant mood. She was known for her hatefulness. No one knew the reason why especially the granddaughter that had been abandoned by her daughter and her husband. Their divorce left her with the evidence of her failed marriage and her daughter's also. She was Janelle. The only offspring of her daughter Patricia and the only grandchild she would ever have. Annie was a challenge to most. She lived her life her way. She did not fear anything or anyone; in fact, everyone was afraid of her. She ranted and raved until she got what she wanted. There was no telling her no. She was not affectionate. She did not show love, and many thought she did not even know how. This was evident in the way she raised her daughter and now her granddaughter.

Her granddaughter was sure she never loved her. She was the victim of her physical abuse. Her grandmother would get off work and come in as hot as hell fire and brimstone cussing and fussing about any and everything. She worked hard and had what she wanted in life but there was a void that no one could fill. She seemed to take it out on the one person that was left to live with her - her granddaughter.

Annie managed to plant a massive garden every year. This year being no different, she had her granddaughter to help with preparing the ground for planting. She always paid one of the neighbors to come and till the ground. She would go over it and pull up all the clumps of dirt that she could not break up with her garden hoe. Every day after she got off work, she went to work in the garden. It had to be planted to help save money. She was not being given anything to take care of her grandchild. Her daughter was off in Atlanta pursuing a modeling career. Her father was depressed and locked in

86

their former home amongst the over whelming amount of stuff he had begun to hoard. His abandonment of his daughter and the rejection of her existence was unexplainable. Neither contacted their daughter.

So, the evenings began in the heat and in the field. It was if she had to earn her keep. She was a slave to her grandmother Annie and Janelle would be responsible for picking up and tossing the larger clumps over to the side in the grassy area that contoured the soon to be garden. This day, Janelle was not moving fast enough the next act would leave a scar on the young girl's soul as well as a mark on her back. Annie began to rant and rave about how lazy she was. She began to cuss and fuss about how slow Janelle was moving. This went on for a few minutes amongst the instructions of what heavy clumps of dirt to get and throw away. As Janelle bent over to reach down and get the large clump of dirt and take it to the perimeter of the garden, she felt a sharp searing pain in her back. She thought, "Did she just dig into my back with the garden hoe?" She was not imagining things. Amid the cussing and fussing that all the neighbors could hear, she took the garden hoe and dug into the back of her granddaughter as if she was the land she was preparing. The pain was unlike anything Janelle had ever experienced. She felt like a slave, only fit to work the field and listen to the constant negative words her own grandmother would speak over her and her life. This place seemed to be a permanent prison of which there no escape. The neighbors could hear the beatings. They listened every day to the cries of the eight-year-old child who was the unwilling victim of her grandmother's abuse. They listened every day to the cries for help, yet they closed their windows and doors in an effort to pretend that the beatings and abuse were not happening right next door. They would not dare call the police; If Annie ever found out who called she would try her best to kill them. Her only relief and release seemed to come from the torment she unleashed everyday upon her granddaughter. Even though everybody knew about her hateful, mean ways they dare not cross her. They feared that she would unleash the same upon them. The granddaughter paid the price to come from Greensboro to cross Annie.

Although Janelle was seven when her parents broke up, by ten she had been the futile pain of their failure forced to reside with the angry and bitter mother of her mom. In the years that she would live there, others would come and go. Foster kids would be taken away because of just how mean she was, and the ones assigned to stay with her would report the mean nature of Annie and be removed. No one would dare take the granddaughter; she took all the beatings, cursings, word curses spoken over her and the lashing that they could not take. It was illegal for her to abuse them so the one person who was not under the protection took the beatings for everyone else was Janelle. How she survived being beat daily is a mystery till this day.

Janelle

This child was born to two parents who had some deep seeded issues as a result of their divorce. These issues initiated the rejection of their only child born to their union. What did this look like to their child? It did not paint a pretty picture! She had grown accustomed to the life of both parents being present. She went to private school. She was not destined to be a statistic. She was not created to life a life of sacrifice, struggle and lack. These were foreign to her but a lifestyle she would become comfortable in for many years to come. The life she was about to embark upon was a fast track straight to hell. She would experience more by the age of thirteen than most people by the age of seventy. She witnessed her mother pimping herself out just to get drugs. The parties where the pills were readily available and access to drugs were in every room. Drug dealers threw house parties back in those days-loud music, alcohol and whatever drug of choice was available. The drug dealer, the mother's boyfriend was rich. He was with was one of the largest suppliers around. He ran his own business and it was very lucrative, so much so that he could run the income from his drugs right into his business and no one even question it. His income from being a carpenter and builder was more than enough to run his drug money through. His local sponsor that brought him to the states, mentor and friend was a doctor; he was also a back-up plan. Their relationship became toxic and dangerous. Physical confrontations and stalking became a regular part of their interactions.

Mother had broken up with her supplier and that led her down a path that included many creative and promiscuous ways to fund her drug habit. The drug dealer always took care of her daughter as if she was his own. No matter what her mother did or become he was still fond of her daughter. He did not let the issues her mother had stop him from taking care of her child. From the point he finally left mother alone, the daughter would have to seek him out before she would ever speak to him again, when she was well into her forties. He was the same. Still absent and leaving daughter feeling rejected by another potential parent. Her mom was still the same as well, but the daughter had changed.

The Impact

Janelle was broken by the lifestyles she had been exposed to. She was a pile of ruins and could not get her life together. She was mauled from their rejection and spent many years going in circles looking for the love and acceptance they would not give her. Years and years passed and one failed relationship after another began to be her cycle; her pain became the way she survived; she even planned for the moment that her relationships would fail. She did not see what love looked like and In between the lines there was no secret message. Her grandmother, father and mother made it perfectly clear that she was not a priority and none of them wanted her. This pain played out for many years as she searched for the acceptance of others at the sacrifice of herself. She laid aside what she wanted thinking that pleasing people would help her fill the void. She did everything they wanted just to feel loved. She went hard at anything she did just to prove she was worthy. Love was replaced by pain. That is how she learned to love. It had to hurt; if it did hurt, there was no love in it. She spent the bulk of her life under this pattern and cycle of abuse and pain. Thinking it was honorable to hurt, she lived like her grandmother and her mother, bitter and broken was the plight she was left to live out.

She became another statistic repeating the same mistakes that her parents not realizing she did not have to! She had no clue how to fight and win. She did not even know she had permission to stand up and win! She made bad relationship choice after bad relationship choice. She was looking for a man to be the reflection of her. She never found it. Her search continued to be active as well as misguided. She should have been preparing the very best version of herself while waiting on her husband. She began to act as if everything was ok, but she was coming unglued on the inside. For years she would contact her parents and share the things she was doing. Her father would always disregard her and begin to talk about himself and his glory days in ministry. Her mother refused to take any of her calls. She had moved and got a new telephone number and her mother was too stubborn to dial it. She had two nervous breakdowns and several meltdowns. The recovery would need to be orchestrated by God. She had to want it. That was the only way God was going to rid her of her demons.

The Recovery

90

Janelle did not know what but knew there had to be a better way. She looked at tv and saw love in so many shows and though that was love. She did not know how to achieve that kind of love and her family did not look like theirs. She did not come from the money they had. She was broke and broken; so was her mother and so was her father. Although her mother's mom was not broke, she was so broken it did not matter how much money she had. She could not buy what she had been missing all her life, happiness. This went on into her adult life and carried over into her marriage and the relationship with her children. The fractured little girl was now a broken woman looking for healing. Partially, it was found in the home and arms of her other grandparents - the parents of her father. They saw the damage that their divorce did to Janelle and when she finally arrived on their doorstep at age nine as a runaway and realized something had to be done. They took her to her father, but this was short lived. Janelle had two nervous breakdowns at the hands of her biological parents who never wanted her after their divorce. The road ahead would be long and hard, but victory was coming!

It would be years later before this story would come to an end - coming to a positive end was a far stretch! However, at the time of this writing of this book, Janelle was called to come and minister at her Aunt's church. She had been forewarned that there would be a time when she would have to go back to where the pain originated and minister. She had to go to Siler City, North Carolina. She had to go back home to tell her full testimony; one that would set the entire area on edge. They could not handle her truth. The reality that she had to go back to the place of such pain was unthinkable, but she could have never turned it down. God had another plan and her obedience was necessary for it to come to pass. For years Janelle felt her parents abandoned her and were never there to protect her from the pain life dealt her; much of which was because of them. All she wanted was to be loved and accepted by the ones who created her. She had searched for their love in everybody she met. Now, God was about to change things.

God was specific with His instructions. Janelle had to take the speaking engagement to preach at her Aunt's church. More clearly than before, she could hear what God was telling her to do next – she had to contact and invite her parents. She had to reach out to the mother she had not spoken to for over twenty years and the father she has not seen since he left. She was afraid she would be met with the opposition of rejection again. God knew whatever He asked of her she would do it because of her love for Him, even if it hurt. She had her daughter to call her mother because she did not have her birth mother's phone number; she was nervous but proceeded anyway. Her daughter reached her mom and had a brief conversation. Quickly her daughter got to the reason for the call. "Grandma, my mom wants to talk to you ok?" Janelle greeted her mother and invited her to church with her Sunday. Much to her surprise, her mother accepted the invite. She was excited and decided that she was going to church with her daughter and family. Janelle left a message for her father through her Aunt. At the time of this writing he had not responded. Janelle's faith in God remained strong and confident. After that call Janelle spoke with her mother almost daily. Her mother fixed Sunday dinner after the service and she has made several visits to see her mother since then.

The relationship she always wanted with her mother was no longer clouded by drugs. Her mother had forgot the reason why she had not heard from her daughter for over twenty years. She had forgot and Janelle forgave. Janelle decided to leave it there and enjoy her mother. After years of rejection she had forgiven her parents. Although the task was hard, it was reflective of the God in her. Her relationship with him was so important to her that she would not allow anything or anyone to cause any sort of separation to come between her and the God she served. All the anger was gone. All the hurting places were healed. She prayed to God that he would give her parents the opportunity to know him and turn their lives around. Her mother shared how she was finished with drugs and that she was saved. This was the absolute joy Janelle had desired to feel. She had prayed that even if they never become the parents, that they would at least give their hearts to the Lord and it finally happened. She prayed, "Lord if You have to save them and take them, I am ok with that. I do not want them to miss out on you. They cannot go back and retrieve time for me, but my heart wants to make sure they don't miss out on a relationship with you." Janelle was ready to spend the rest of her life without her parents alive if it meant saving them and taking them. She was ok with not having the relationship she desired with them if they would just give their lives to the Lord. God had a plan that was far greater. He gave Janelle her mother back. At the time of this writing, she is still believing God for her dad. Janelle is walking confidently in who God created her to be! She is finally at peace. Peace being, nothing missing and nothing broken. God did not reject her and that is all the acceptance she needed!

Ciltona Cawthorne

Ciltona Cawthorne is a native New Yorker. She is a gifted poet, an entrepreneur, motivational speaker, spoken word artist, model and author. She loves movies, dance, the theatre, good conversation and Cappuccino. Ciltona is a warrior woman for God, who comes from a long line of storytellers with entrepreneurial mindsets. Ciltona admires her daughter Ebony, a 2018 graduate from the UNCSA school of film for her grace, strength, intellect and creativity. She believes that children can be mentored to achieve excellence using the arts.

Ciltona Cawthorne is passionate about mentoring youth and helping women to be inspired and encouraged. Her poetry teaches that all of God's children are gifted and we are not limited by our past. She draws her strength from God's promises, love, grace and mercy.

Ciltona is working on a book of inspirational poetry, and a children's book, both which will be published in early 2020. She currently resides in Greensboro, NC.

Ciltona's Dedication

This chapter is dedicated to my darling daughter Ebony. My greatest joy has been the blessing to be your mother. I love you dearly, and you inspire me constantly. You made me become stronger, and braver than I ever thought possible. Continue to dream big and walk in your power and gifts to glorify God!!

"Every great dream begins with a dreamer. Always remember, you have within you the strength, the patience, and the passion to reach for the stars to change the world."
-Harriet Tubman

Connect with Ciltona

Ciltona., Your Encouragement Sister

Phone: (336) 365-8634

CHAPTER 6

Be Encouraged

I did not know I was gifted. I did not know I was strong. I did not know my worth. I only felt beautiful, valued and loved when I was with my family. I loved school academically but socially school became a nightmare for me at age 11. From sixth grade and all through high school I was bullied and harassed with mean-spirited name calling and complexion and body shamming by people that looked like me. My grandmother said, "your color don't mean they your kind." I would sit for hours and try to figure out what was wrong with me and why someone was always picking on me. I ran track in college because I had developed the speed and skill from running home every day in sixth grade as I was chased by bullies. So, remember my sisters those hard, uncomfortable situations will develop your gifts and strengths. Look for what is being developed.

I had my sixteenth birthday party with my best friend because our birthdays were six days apart. She was liked by the popular crowd and so, in my twisted logic, they would come to our party because they liked her and then they would like me too; what they did was come late, without any gifts, ate all the food, cake and left. As they left laughing, they talked loudly about how lame our party was. I was crushed and cannot tell you how long I cried. That was when I decided to become popular and recreate myself into the club queen, "Silky Love", through makeup, promiscuity, cigarettes, drugs and alcohol. I told myself I was gorgeous, sexy and brilliant and I acted the part. I struggled with low self-esteem and suicidal thoughts and looked for outside validation. In my drug-induced insanity, I became popular through my sexual escapades. I graduated from high school and sold drugs to support my club lifestyle. I was extremely excited to go to college for the real partying and to find some college men to have sex with. I equated my increased fornicating and group drug use with acceptance.

As a college freshman, I created a sex survey for my writing class project and got an A on it. I used the survey to find the men I wanted to have sex with. It is by the grace of God that I do not have AIDS. I lived for sex and the next great party and truly believed that drugs enhanced everything. I dropped out of college because I needed more money to support my party lifestyle. I did not see the necessity for a college degree. I hung out Wednesday through Saturday, and slept all day Sunday, to rest up for my busy party week ahead. I had two jobs and sold marijuana for hang out money. At work, I smoked drugs on my lunch hour, sipped wine with my cheeseburger and had cocktails after work on the way to a club. In my delusions, I believed I was incredibly sophisticated and successful. I took great pride in the fact that I was not a fall down sloppy drunk. I shopped at Lord and Taylor's, wore designer labels and had a lot of unprotected sex. I worked to increase my designer wardrobe and my sexual conquests but not my finances nor my self-esteem. My identity was wrapped up in my clubbing, lifestyle of sex and drugs and the crowd I hung out with. I craved the validation and acceptance I felt from my sexual escapades and the sexy persona I created. I was sought after and desired and it felt wonderful. I had discovered my voice – I was loud, vulgar and could curse out a truck driver! My family loved me, but they were alcoholics and drug users and I hid my pain well. I created nothing of value, and I wasted time and money. I did not know that there was more to life than going from one high to the next. I did not see anything wrong with the way I was living.

When I had my daughter, I understood that my decisions would affect her, so I enrolled my daughter in Catholic school, and I began my search to find her a church.

98

I wanted her to have the Christian foundation that I had, because although all the adults in my family were substance abusers who were in pain and hung out every weekend, they sent me to Sunday school every Sunday. I did not feel that I was lacking anything, so I made a list of churches with travel times so we could visit and I pick one. I had us join the first church on my list even though it was not the closest. I was impressed because they sang a hymn I remembered from my childhood. I went to new member's class, had my child baptized and left church every week with a terrible headache. I was in church but had no relationship with God.

Fast-forward 5 years and I had relocated to Greensboro, NC. My daughter had settled into high school and the church youth department. I still felt like an outsider - either I was surrounded by singles years younger than me, clique' cute people or these super marvelous married couples. I did not want to be married, I just wanted to find my crew, my circle, who would listen to me and I could hang out with. My daughter and I were in our first drama ministry play in our new church and I was so excited!

As rehearsals progressed, I struggled with memorizing my lines. I was the oldest member of the cast and had the most lines. I had to stop my daughter from beating up fellow cast members who were making fun of me for my inability to remember my lines. My young queen was a warrior and wanted to defend me, but through God's grace I was able to truthfully tell her that being talked about and ridiculed did not bother me. I felt sorry for those that got enjoyment at another person's expense. I used those incidents as examples to teach my daughter how not to act. We must uplift, edify and reflect Christ. The week before our Pastor had preached from Joshua 1:9, and the scripture began to have a growing impact on me.

⁹ Have I not commanded you? Be strong and courageous! Do not be terrified or dismayed (intimidated), for

**the LORD your God is with you wherever you go." -
Joshua 1:9**

In this verse, God tells us to be strong and courageous three times, to emphasize this phrase to Joshua. But why? Joshua was not a kid and had been trained under Moses for years. God repeated this scripture because of the benevolent Father that God is. He gives us what we need, and Joshua needed to hear and be reminded to be strong and courageous for the task at hand, and these words were included for us generations later for times when we would be given tasks, challenges and divine assignments that may appear to be unachievable. Just as God poured into Joshua with the words be strong and courageous, I received encouragement and was empowered by these words also.

God was preparing Joshua. In His infinite wisdom God spoke those words of life, direction and encouragement to Joshua, because it was what Joshua needed. It was what I needed during that season where I was doubting myself in the play and in my life. My warrior queen ran lines with me constantly, and I carried a copy of the script everywhere I went. I was strong and courageous because God told me I was, and I now believed I was after decades of low-self-esteem and self-doubt. I learned everyone's lines in the play, not just mine; God was preparing me for being on the mic.

The poetry I write is me speaking to encourage myself. I speak from my dark places, from my disappointment, from my self-doubt and from my anger. I write to tell myself what I need to hear, and I echo who God says I am. Lines drop and I know God dropped that piece to comfort and encourage me and this is what I share when I am on the mic. Have you ever just sat down and cried because you know you messed up, you know you missed it and are left feeling alone and broken with no way out? I was in church and active in ministry only to go home to curl up, cry and scream inside for someone to fix it. I begged God to send me someone to help me, see me and love me but no one came to wipe my tears and tell me how wonderful I was that day. I found myself instead, wiping my face and tucking my baby in bed and reminding her of how wonderful and brilliant she was and whose she was. When I looked in the mirror, I did not see someone I loved; I looked at my reflection with disapproval and only saw my flaws.

God is so amazing. I realized that God had waited for me to find Him and He loves me in spite of myself and my past promiscuous lifestyle. God does not consult our past to determine our future. The fact that He has blessed me to speak life to women and encourage them through my poetry still amazes me. My poems come forth as I encourage myself. On some days it still takes a push for me to face the world, because of ailments, sadness and loneliness. If I focus on my limitations, feelings of inadequacy begin to creep in. I begin to feel disheartened and disappointed with myself because of bad decisions that I made; but when I focus on the goodness of God and His grace, mercy and love I become empowered, encouraged and strengthened. I know my current situation is not my destiny. I know I am a gifted poetess and motivational speaker who is called to encourage women. I know I am not average! I will not speak average! I will no longer hide my brilliance and I will not hide from my destiny! I do not need to fit in because God created me to stand out! I was created by the Master Creator, in His image, to have dominion and be His representation on this earth.

When I stopped accepting people's limited beliefs about me and my identity, I started to break the strongholds over me. What I do now I have always done but now, I embrace my gifts and my divine assignment to inspire, motivate and encourage women to see themselves as God sees them. In hindsight I see that I have always had the gift

101

to encourage. I am your Encouragement sister, here to show you there is a better way and that we are fearfully and wonderfully made. Even when you are having one of those not so great days it is always possible to make it better and when you need encouragement, God is always there with His unconditional love for you. Do not listen to the naysayers. Haters will hate. Your divine assignment is just that, your assignment. Talk to the Lord, spend time with God in His word and in prayer and God with bless you with discernment to recognize your support team. Your Heavenly Father will send you who and what you need to fulfill your divine assignment. The more time you spend with God and dwell in His word the stronger and more courageous you will become. Courage and strength are benefits of spending time with God. You are beautiful, brilliant and powerful, you were not created to be a victim. You were created in the image of God to be victorious, believe it, embrace in and walk in it. Read that again, now say it aloud to yourself in the mirror. You are beautiful, brilliant and powerful!

A Love Letter

This is a love letter to you my dear sisters.

I am my hero, the one who comes to save the day, Yes I can ride a horse so I can come charging in on my stallion poised with sword drawn as I ride, (because I'm bad like that) ready to fight. Time to swing and slice, take no prisoners, no holds barred. I am mighty, strong and empowered by my omnipotent God. I was created for victorious conquest. In the action movie of my life I kick in the door, guns a blazing taking out bad guys. I love a good action movie, when the woman is the hero, and doesn't have to be saved by a man. I'm just being real! You have what it takes to be your own hero, be who you need, get what you need, learn what you need to and make it happen. Be your own hero, embrace the warrior that you are. I need you to get this! You are gifted and you were created by God to be successful and wealthy. God gave us dominion, so walk in that!! Stay humble sis, God loves you and wants you to prosper, so He has given you power, intellect and gifts to create wealth. I dream big, I trust God and I grind hard!! I go to work every day and when I get off from my job, I go to work for myself and I grind hard to make it happen. I grind hard to create and build my empire that will bless others with my products, services and my story of triumph. I was not created to struggle; I was not created to embrace lack and wear it like a cozy sweater. I refuse to be comfortable where I was not created to be. So yes, I am creating my empire to leave as a legacy for those that come after me and my legacy will also be a tribute to those that came before me and paved the way. I am brilliant, beautiful and a masterpiece created by God in His image to create, have dominion and abundance.

And so are you.

I am brilliant, beautiful and a masterpiece created by God in His image to create, have dominion and abundance.

And so are you.

Much love,

Ciltona- Your Encouragement Sister

"When hard pressed, I cried to the Lord; he brought me into a spacious place. The Lord is with me; I will not be afraid. What can mere mortals do to me?"

Psalm 118:5-6 NIV

Dominique S. Cunningham

Dominique S Cunningham is a native of Greensboro, North Carolina. She is the oldest of three girls and loves her sisters dearly. She is a servant leader within the church where God has gracefully placed her. She has worked in the customer service field for 12 years and is a forthcoming pharmacy technician. She has earned credentials in early childhood and cherishes the memories she has made over the years caring for children and changing the lives of people one service at a time. Dominique has been active in ministry since the age of thirteen and truly has a heart for God's people. Dominique serves her Executive Pastor Brandi Rojas faithfully as armor bearer, she is an intercessor and Youth Group Assistant at Maximizing Life Family Worship Center in Greensboro, North Carolina. Dominique is the mother of two beautiful girls and is currently planning to marry the love of her life. Dominique is advocate for children with special needs and plan to write a book in the future encouraging the parents of these children. She has received several certificates and completed many assignments in ministry over the years with the help of God. She has recently decided to go back to school and further her education because of the most recent mandate God has given her.

Above everything in life, Dominique cherish the gifts that God has given her in the form of children and is working to be the mother and woman of God that He has called her to be. The love she has for ministry and family helped to birth out a real desire to pray. Dominique prays daily and wholeheartedly believing that prayer changes things for the better. She is on fire for God and excited about walking through those pearly gates and hearing, " Well done my good and faithful servant."

Dominique's Dedication

To my mother Regina who has always backed me and supported me in all of my endeavors:

My mother did not just say "I love you" but showed it in her actions daily. My mother made many sacrifices and worked hard to ensure that my siblings and I was well taken care of. She set an excellent example as a mother and has made my parenting journey much easier. She has a heart of gold and spreads love and joy everywhere she goes. She is beautiful, loyal and resilient. I thank God all the time for the gift He gave me in the form of my mother. I am living my life as a Queen just as she taught me and promise to make her proud. Regina Cunningham you're the absolute best! May God smile down on you forever and always.

Connect with Dominique
Email: QueenD_cunningham@gmail.com.
Phone: (919) 694 3537

CHAPTER 7

Sufficient Grace

Who would have thought that the ugliest part of my life would be a powerful part of my testimony? It all started in my tenth-grade year of high school when I got my first real crush. There was a tall, handsome, funny, well-dressed guy that I could not keep my eyes off of. We shared the same lunch hour and I would see him passing through the hallway. He had my attention in such a way that I started taking the long way to the buses in the afternoon so I could walk past his locker. I would get a window seat every time and gaze out the window smiling from ear to ear as if we were having a full-blown conversation. Before I knew it, I was telling my best friend about him and writing his name in my journal with hearts; he appeared to be the perfect person. I admired so many things about him and was just waiting for the opportunity to present my list to him. Several weeks had passed and I was still undecided on what to say or how I wanted to say "it", so I just did what I knew to do - I pranced around each day looking pretty, smiling big, lips shining and glossed up, every hair in place and with my shoes laced! My non-verbal communication was on point! I was styling and profiling! My friends and I sat in the same place every day - directly across from him. He was the comedian of the group, and we were always laughing. Some might call us "ear hustlers". That school year quickly ended, and we had only two conversations. Both occasions we talked about cards because that is what he and his friends did during their spare time. That year was a good one for me; I did well academically and had some eye candy to help make my day a little sweeter. I finished with a bang and was preparing for the eleventh grade. I left the tenth grade hoping that "he" would come back to the same school too. Being the oldest child, I had many responsibilities around the house and automatically knew to keep a close watch on my little sisters. Every summer I did the same thing, after breakfast and chores I made sure my sisters and I were dressed and ready to spend the day outside. If we were not on vacation, we were outside at the neighborhood park or pool. I was the child that knew what my mom liked and had no problem doing it, not to mention the fact that doing so would allow us to go outside and enjoy the day. My mom and I have always had a good relationship, a close relationship, until I fell in love or should I say, I thought that I was experiencing love.

The second week of August came, and I was beyond ready to go back to school. We had already taken care of the clothes, shoes, and school supplies and I was anxious to know who my classmates were. Did I have any classes with "him"? Was he coming back to our school this year? The first day of school, I was looking good and feeling good and it all worked to my advantage! I had two classes with him, and we shared the same lunch hour. Excitement and nerves took over and I knew that this was it! Becoming good friends with Josh was my goal for the first quarter of school. I sat down and came up with a plan one afternoon because I was bored and had nothing better to do. I said, "Let me use my intelligence to reel him in." From that day forward I was attentive in class; I was studying hard and passing every test with excellence and even went to the white board and solved problems a few times which I hated doing. It was truly a stretch for me, but I pushed through it. (We all know that the popular guys, the center of attention, easy on the eye type fellas like the pretty, smart girls and I was definitely her and she was me.)

I walked in class early one Tuesday morning and to my surprise Josh was sitting in my seat. With butterflies in my stomach, I nicely asked him to move. He smiled big, put his headphones in and pretended not to hear me; I smiled back and asked again to which he responded back with a big "NO". My heart dropped to my stomach the moment I realized that he was playing/flirting with me and that he had purposely sat in my seat and wanted to pick a fight with me. Yes, me! I was caught off guard and really did not know what to do; I was like a deer caught in headlights. Eventually he got up and went to his seat, but he left his notebook and told me to read what he had written on the last page. We were low-key and under the radar with our dating, but I loved everything about it. In the notebook, he asked me one simple question and told me if the answer to the question was "yes", to leave my phone number. He asked if I liked him; yes or no. I wrote back and told him that I did like him and that I had my eye on him since last year. I gave him my phone number and he wasted no time in using it; from that day forward, I was stuck to his hip. We were talking on the phone every afternoon, began writing love notes and passed them back and forth every other day. We purposely stayed after school for the same tutorial sessions. We were "vibing" and I was so happy to finally have a story to tell my friends. He was the very first person I ever dated, and I was feeling like a late bloomer because my peers had stories galore with their "girl guess what I did last night" conversations. I would usually just smile and nod when it was my turn to tell, but now, things were different.

The school year was coming to an end and Josh and I was sitting down talking about how glad we were that he had a car and began planning things to do over the summer. As the days drew closer, I became more emotionally attached to him because I knew the daily conversation and connection was ending. Although we had planned to see each other over the summer I knew it would not be often because my mother was all about the "books before boys" lifestyle. My mother strongly believed in education and took pride in the fact that her daughters were not fast and sexually active like some of our peers. I was nervous about even mentioning him to my mom and openly told Josh that the freedom he had in his household, I did not. On the last Friday of the school year,

Josh and I decided to skip class and go have sex. I was afraid but I was ready; the last couple of months he had done so many nice things for me and his touch was always so warm and welcoming. I loved hugging him and loved it even more when he would kiss me before saying good-bye after school some days. We had sex in the car that day and everything went well. I went home, showered and played things off as normal but there was a part of me that felt bad. I had a strong conscience even as a young girl because I had already given my life to Christ so inwardly, I was a mess.

I continued to talk to him on the phone and we hooked up several times over the summer. I would go to the mall on weekends to spend time with him and even jump out of windows late at night. There was something about him that I really liked and could not get enough of. I introduced him to my mom and sisters a couple of times but did most of my connecting with him in secret. I thought I was grown. I was in my last year of high school and had a man of my own. Everything was working in my favor until I found out I was pregnant the third month of my senior year. After being sick for a few days my mom took me to the doctor and they gave us the results right away, "Ms. Cunningham congratulations! You are pregnant!" That was terrible news for us, and I was devastated. My mother, who I admired so much, even to this day kept her composure and released her tears in the car. There I was, a seventeen-year-old pregnant twelfth grader. It was a day that I will never forget. I was lost for words and I felt extremely nauseous, but I found a little bit of peace knowing that Josh was my only partner and knew that he would have my back through this. The first thing I did after my mother sat me down and had that "mother to mother" talk was call Josh; I could tell he was disappointed and shocked from the response he gave me. He did not receive my words at all and a part of me knew that I had made a mistake. The conversation got heated, and he made me

110

feel like I had gotten myself pregnant; he yelled at me and I yelled back as tears streamed down my face. Just like that, things had changed and took a downward turn in our relationship. Depression crept up on me I had started to regret the baby and all of our sexual encounters after just a couple of days of finding out. It hurts when you are ignored by the person whose attention is the only thing you want in the world.

Going to school was hell for me because Josh and I had completely stopped communicating. We could barely stand the site of each other, and to make matters worse, I found out he had another girl at school pregnant too; everything but suicide crossed my mind. How could I be so stupid? How could I be so stupid enough to give my prize away and to sneak behind my mother's back and lie to the one person who has held me down from day one? I was disgusted with myself and had thought about dropping out of school. I was embarrassed and was talked about day in and day out. A rumor started going around the school that I was a whore and was trying to trap Josh because not many people knew about our rendezvous. He was well liked and known around school and I was the girl who popped up pregnant by him. I received so many dirty looks and heard so many untruths that I no longer felt worthy; I even stopped caring about my education.

My mother tried her hardest to console me, but I rejected her because my mind kept telling me that I deserved this pain and brought it upon myself. I was surrounded by the love of my family my entire pregnancy, but I still felt alone. I would literally have to wake up an extra thirty minutes early for school every day so I could get my crying and hateful words out. I truly believe that words have power and here I was, speaking all of these negative things over myself and everybody concerning the matter. I prayed that Josh would break a limb or get into a bad car accident so he would need me, and I could boldly fail him like he did me. I was in a dark place and had lost all faith until God sent me a message through the cafeteria lady. She could see the hurt in my eyes and pulled me to the side one day to encourage me. She said, "God's grace is sufficient for you and you will make it through this." That sentence was needed and sparked something up deep down inside me. A light came on in my head and I decided to open my daily devotional that I had put on the shelf to collect dust. I was feeding myself the word of God and focusing less on the negativity. I repented for my sins and changed my way of thinking. All the things that I learned in church over the years were rising back up in me. Satan was fighting me hard and even using other people, including Josh's other child's mother to come after me, but I remained levelheaded through it all. I reminded myself of what the lunch lady had said, "God's grace is sufficient" for everything I needed in this season."

My due date was approaching, and I was preparing to leave school and go on homebound. Josh and I still were not speaking. He had no idea about the sex of the baby or when she was due, but all was well with me. I was glad to be leaving that school for good. The DNA results were heavy on my mind and I could not wait to finally prove that I was not a whore and that Josh did sleep with me whether he wanted to admit it or not. I really wanted to show him the results because the naïve part of me believed a man could not comfortably live with himself and not take care of his children. I was young and dumb and had no idea how parenting really worked. There were many times that I put all my hope and faith in him after the baby was born and he failed me badly. My big heart and my love for people, especially him, had me living in a fantasy world. On May 15 at 12:43 pm, I gave birth to a beautiful baby girl. The Lord God Almighty covered me through it all and my family flooded the hospital the entire day. They were bringing the baby and I all kinds of treats and heart felt gifts. You would have thought that I would have been happy, but I was not. All kinds of evil thoughts and feelings came over me instantly after I delivered the baby and looked in her eyes. She was gorgeous but her eyes reminded me of the fact that I was now connected to her father for the next eighteen years. She had the same eyes as him and I could not help but to face the fact that he had failed me yet again. He was not there for the delivery and had no idea that I had been in labor for the past fourteen hours. I did not try to reach out to him before going to the hospital because I knew by his actions that he did not care. We were not a priority to him. I was heartbroken all over again and depression showed up, except this time, it came for my life. I wrote a "goodbye letter" to my family and stole pills from my grandmother after being discharged from the hospital, but God would not allow me to follow through with it. Instead, He had me trash my entire plan, from the intent, to the letter and the pills, and sent a comforting word from my dear sister in Christ to get me back on the right track.

My mother and I reached out to him after the DNA testing was done to let him know that he was 99.9% the father. We showed him the paper, but that news still went in one ear and out the other. The first two years was the hardest for me because I refused to accept the truth for what it was. I reached out to him time after time. I showed up at his house but could not get any consistent help or financial support. My heart kept telling me to be patient, to try it again and to put myself in his shoes but that was all a set up for failure; his mind was made up and he was not willing to be a full-time father. I was exhausted with the process and needed the tiny bit of energy that I had left to care for my child, so I took my hands off the situation and allowed the state to get involved at that point.

Parenting got easier for the both of us after about

five or six rough years. We tried to get along and be social hundreds of times; we would go a few weeks with no arguments or fallouts, and I would be so sure that our hateful, disrespectful days were over. I would be smiling on the inside and ready to jump for joy then BOOM, something strange would happen. We were still sexually active so there was a soul tie that neither one of us wanted to accept but boy oh boy did it have me acting out of character. I would say that him doing whatever with whomever was okay as long as he took care of our child but that was not the case. The text messages and hickeys that I was finding had me feeling angry. We were playing a dangerous game with each other and I had to find the strength to let go. I had to let him, the emotions and the confusion go. I struggled doing that because I knew that he had a good heart and through all the pain and darkness, which I personally experienced, there was a little bit of love still left and I was sure of that. There were countless good days and my mind did not want to forget them. He was my homie, lover and enemy all wrapped up into one.

I was really in need of a friend to slap some sense into me. I was behaving like a young, reckless girl with no home training or self-respect and that was not me; with all the teaching and nurturing my mother did while raising us I was acting clueless. Jesus Christ was my only hope because I was too ashamed to let anyone in on what I was really going through. I could not wrap my head around the cycle that we had created or the demons that I let into my life by sleeping with someone who I knew was sleeping with other people. I was feeling sick to my stomach and desperate for a change. I stayed up all night one night praying and travailing before God; I was tired of men after just being involved with that one person and I went searching for the love that only God could give; I wanted that undeniable joy that no human could give me. I had known God to be a way maker

114

because He had been making ways for me since high school; I had seen Him perform many miracles, so I resolved to keep praying and believing that He could do it again. I found myself shouting and leaping in my room and woke the baby up; as soon as she began babbling, I smiled and considered that worship, too! We had a good time and the Lord came down from Heaven to see about me that night. He changed some things deep down inside and I never saw Josh in the same light again; he was not able to get under my skin or between my legs ever again.

I tried to keep myself busy over the years and out of the way. I was trying to redeem myself all by myself until God spoke to me and told me that suffering in silence was a toxic trait of mine. My God and my daughter challenged me to make a change for the better, so I went searching for help and opened up to loved ones and a close friend. I told them what I needed instead of praying that they would notice the change in me and ask. My family was open to helping me and has been our village since day one. They are great people.

Only a true and living God can know exactly what you need before you need it. It was Jesus Christ who laid it on the cafeteria lady's heart to speak to me. It was Jesus who placed those timely words in the devotional book that I had been reading. God placed me in a loving family and knew that I would need their support before I was formed in my mother's womb; He is strategic and the God of His word. Deuteronomy 31:6 (NIV) says this:

Be strong and courageous. Do not be afraid or terrified because of them, for the LORD your God goes with you; He will never leave you nor forsake you."

I stand as a proud witness today to tell you that He keeps His promises. I held on to that scripture and God held on to me! All the real praise and honor goes to God

Almighty for holding my hand on this journey. I do not understand how people could choose not to serve a God like Him. His love and tender mercy are mind blowing and free to all of us. Sexual diseases, suicide, abortion all could have been an option, but God did not allow it to be so. He has forgiven me and allowed me the chance to move forward with a purpose. He has blessed my children and I with a God fearing, loving, hard - working, great cooking man who helps me to view my past as preparation. My fiancé is heaven sent and a reflection of God's love for me. Now, we are planning our wedding and with each day that passes we are allowing God to be the foundation. I am so glad to finally have someone who feels for me what I feel for him. I tell my testimony every chance I get and want every young mother in the world to know that Jesus is the same God today, tomorrow and forever more. If He can do it for me, He can do it for anyone. Do not hesitate to open your mouth and cry out to Him in your time of need because He will surly come see about you and perfect those things that concern you. Be encouraged! Much love!

LaRissa Oxner

 LaRissa Oxner is a published Author, Entrepreneur and Healthcare Professional from Maryland. Known for sharing the good news and positive vibes, her desire to inspire, celebrate, and restore those who feel forgotten or voiceless led her to also begin a career in radio broadcasting. Serving as a community leader in this capacity further developed her skill and love for public speaking. She is passionate about sharing her experiences of being an overcomer to help build and restore communities, families, and individuals.

LaRissa Oxner is a valued and influential ministry leader at Abundant Harvest Ministries, proud member of the Ladies of Radiance Women's Ministry, team member of the Stellar Award Nominated, Awesome God Radio, and cohost of DMV's Talk show of the Year, The Good Life Gospel Show. Her greatest achievement is being the mother of two beautiful daughters.

LaRissa's Dedication

I dedicate this to all mothers who continue to stand in the gap and frontline for their children. You are valuable and treasured. May you continue to be the light your children and family need to shine brightly in their own life. Never give up. Never quit. Never forget to take care of yourselves; mind, body, and spirit. Remember if you aren't good to yourselves you will not be good for anyone else.

I dedicate this to my beautiful daughter Mia. You are my reason for being and becoming. You have come into my life and given me a deeper purpose. Continue to do great things in the earth. You can do ALL things through Christ who is your source and strength. I'm so proud of you. Get it boop boop!

Connect with LaRissa

Facebook : Good News with Rissa
Instagram: ris_rene
Twitter: Ris_reneLo
Website: bit.ly/RisRene

CHAPTER 8

Behind the Veil: Healing after Depression

January 2018 was my time of promise and victory! Yes, out with the old and in with the new. I had recently updated my vision board showcasing my to-do list and all my favorite things- travel, home décor, self-care, health and wellness, inspiration, and motivating quotes. Whew, I was ready to live my best life!

For a few weeks I was very focused on my goals; after all, what is a vision board without taking the necessary steps to see that vision manifest? I would look at my vision board, pray, and check things off my to-do list, however things were not as good as they seemed. Outside I looked happy and successful, but I was a total wreck on the inside. I thought I was over it. My heart was still completely broken and unforgiveness, feelings of disappointment, shame, bitterness and anger began to consume me.

We had been married for almost 8 years and instead of growing together we were growing apart. Marriage is challenging by itself when two people from different worlds are joined together, but when you add other people to the mix it proves fatal. Love turned into lies, communication turned into cursing, time together turned into timidity, and intimacy turned into ignoring one another. We both could feel that the end was drawing near. My husband and I ultimately decided just to make family time with our children top and only priority because that was just easier to handle. If our children were happy, healthy, and loved then we could be too, right? Wrong.

I had reached my breaking point. One night I sat in my car for hours and just screamed and cried. Something had to change. What is a good Christian couple who is active in ministry to do? Of course, go to marriage counseling! We had been in counseling off and on since our first year of marriage and I was tired. No one could tell us how to fix this. It was above us now. God was surely going to have to intervene. "Lord take this cup from me! I cannot live like this and be in authentic relationship with you," I cried. I was very capable of putting on a united church front while ministering - pouring, supporting, praying for, and praising God for the lives of others but I was in a total dark place. Church was my safe haven, but it was also a place I could be invisible. Instead of allowing the moments of fellowship to be my altar of sacrifice, it was my crutch and excuse not to be home working on my marriage. For almost a year no one knew I was not living at home and was sleeping on the couches of different family members. I was not ok, but I made it look good.

Having a blended family is already challenging, but deciding to leave my bonus daughter, who I had raised for over ten years proved to be one of the most difficult decisions I ever had to make, yet it was necessary. Not only was I separated from my husband but at this point my children who were raised together under one roof were now products of a broken household. Several reports show that 50% of all children in the United States will witness the end of a parent's marriage and my family was now added to that percentage.

The first few months of separation was very difficult. I was now a single mom, financially struggling, and my ex and I were not adjusting well to our new normal of co-parenting. Every day was an argument and screaming match for some reason or another. My daughter was used to seeing her father daily and the separation created visitation issues. I had seen this scenario before because I too am a product of a broken home. The difference was that I did not have a solid relationship with my dad, but my daughter did with her father. My daughter was becoming the broken little girl I used to be, and I could not allow it any longer. I began to become bitter and even-more angry.

As parents we must understand that what we do does not just affect us it affects everything and everyone around us.

Maybe I should just go back to him and she could still have a two-parent household? How could I leave the home she had ever known? How could I put her through all this struggle? What kind of emotional damage control could I do to help her see that this was the best decision? Was I being selfish? I could not go back. The marriage was over and going back with a bitter mindset would only make it worst. I cried myself to sleep many nights thinking about whether the decision I made was the right decision for my daughter, but I was good! I was living life focusing on the positive and ignoring all things negative. As long as I was still smiling and self- medicating with busyness everything was alright. Life went on as expected.

"Calm down! You have to calm down," my mother said. "I am calm," I strongly replied. My daughter was giving me her best attitude and I was not having it. I reacted in such a way I could tell she was terrified and for weeks she was very quiet in her responses with me. I could tell something was wrong. I asked, but she would not tell me. I knew it was my reaction toward her during my previous correction and I felt horrible yet again. "I am a single parent, struggling to make life great for us and this is what happens," I tried to convince myself. "She will understand when she gets older."

For healing to take place one must first recognize that they are wounded and that it is okay to ask for help. For so long people have viewed asking for help as a sign of weakness and defeat when in fact it is the very opposite - it makes you strong and victorious. I was not my best self; I was angry, sad, frustrated, hurt. I was a wreck! I was tormenting myself because more than anything I wanted to be a great mother and I did not feel like one. I had failed and I was fearful that I was going to die in this black hole. I had to let this go. I had to find a way to heal and I needed help.

121

"Ask and it will be given to you; seek and you will find; knock and the door will be opened to you. For everyone who asks receives; the one who seeks finds; and to the one who knocks, the door will be opened."

-Matthew 7:7-8 NIV

I recognized that I needed help, but I did not want it from someone who knew me or my situation personally. I wanted to be as anonymous as possible; I was still trying to cover up what was really going on. It was my fourth group session and I was still excited to be in the company of my lady gang friends. It did not bother me that the room was filled with women with ages that ran from mid-forties to late sixties. Some of these ladies were recently separated, some had been married for over thirty years while some had been divorced for a few years. I was the youngest one in the group with the shortest separation story to tell but I felt right at home; this was safe space for me. The feeling of freedom and no judgement flooded my soul because no one knew me and to me, this was part of the health and wellness portion that was on my vision board. After checking in with the receptionist, I sat down as usual and the discussion began. The subject lesson was regarding depression. Immediately I thought I was in the wrong class because I was not depressed, I was angry, and I wanted someone to speak about that.

It has been reported that about 1.5 % of the American population suffer with high functioning depression; it is called dysthymia. These persons do not even realize they are depressed because they appear completely fine – their day-to day functions are maintained, and they are able to keep up with work productivity and relationships. Persons suffering with dysthymia are known not to miss a beat until the day is done. They are faced to look in the mirror and see the reality. They are alone. Those who carry symptoms of High Functioning Depression are plagued by feelings of hopelessness, anxiety, and self-doubt. They constantly critique themselves and seem to doubt their abilities no matter what they succeed. When met with praise, many feel unworthy of recognition.[1]

"Oh my God," I screamed in the middle of the meeting, "I am depressed!" I started hyperventilating and shaking. I was having a major meltdown. I became very, very anxious. Everyone turned and looked at me with concern and rushed to my side to offer support. I was crying uncontrollably. With words that could barely be understood, I said "I cannot be depressed. I do not want to take medication! I do not want to see a psychiatrist! What about my daughter?" One of the leaders of the group grabbed my hand. She looked me in the eyes and said, "LaRissa you will not die here! We are here to help." Immediately, I felt a peace and a calm come over me. I was not alone. I was surrounded by people that understood and I no longer had to hide behind the veil. "Ok," I whispered; I was finally ready to do the work that would bring about my healing.

Healing began when I let go of my pride, took off the mask and acknowledged that I was NOT okay and needed help. I have been known as the strong one all my life and I was tired. I would not stay stuck in finding out that I was showing signs of depression, but rather reverse the signs; I decided that depression was not who I was and I was not going to allow my new normal of being a single mom rage fear and war in my life. That confession catapulted me into healing; I made it through this. It was a test of my faith, my strength, and my character, but I made it out in VICTORY!

Behind a smile tells the story of what was, what is, and what is to become. There were so many times I had

---

[1] http://www.betterhelp.com

cried myself to sleep because my heart was hurting so bad. The truth is, new tears and restless nights have happened since those times before, but rest assure that joy showed up in the morning. For some, morning is when the alarm clock goes off and daylight shows up in the sky, but I have come to remind you that morning is whenever you decide it is time for the sun to shine in your life. Time does not dictate when joy should show up in your life. When you are sick and tired of being sick and tired you will know what time it truly is.

Greater is coming for me and I pray that you know that greater is coming for you as well. Go on and be great!

LaTasha Watson Tisdale

LaTasha Watson Tisdale is a native of Greensboro, North Carolina, where she currently resides. She is the seventh of eight children born to the late Billy and Ada A. Watson. Tisdale received her Associate Degree in Early Childhood Education. She has been working in Child Care as an Administrative Assistant, a Lead Teacher, and now as an ACES Group Leader for over twelve years.

Tisdale is an active member of REACH Ministry in Greensboro, North Carolina. She serves God's Kingdom as a member of the Church Choir, the Hospitality Committee, and the Women's Ministry. She is also a Co-Advisor/Facilitator for the Children/Youth Ministry and one of the Children's Sunday School Teachers.

LaTasha Tisdale is blessed to share this life with her amazing husband of 15 years, Mr. Darryl T. Tisdale, also known as **#TeamTisdale**. This God-ordained dynamic duo are new and upcoming multiprenuers. #TeamTisdale are the CEOs of a multifaceted company called, Team Tisdale, Inc. which was created to serve the community with Christian-based, high quality childcare, soul-enriching travels, "sugar-free and yummy, energized and focus" meal replacements and teas, and amazing Christian entertainment.

LaTasha's Dedication

To the love of my life, Darryl T. Tisdale, thank you for being a daily representation of God's unconditional love. To my amazingly phenomenal late parents, Billy and Ada A. Watson, thank you for all the love and life lessons. Thank you for molding me into the "Strong" woman that I am today. I love you all...Today, Forever and Always!

Connect with LaTasha

Soul Enriched Travels
919.307.9574
Legacy Building: bit.ly/SoulEnrichedTravelsBiz
Booking: bit.ly/SoulEnrichedTravels

Soul Enrichment Nutrition
919.307.9574
www.soulenrichment.goherbalife.com

CHAPTER 9
"The Strong One"

Strength. What is it? According to the *Merriam-Webster Dictionary*, strength is "the quality or state of being physically strong; and the ability to resist being moved or broken by a force."[2] What is even more interesting it that the dictionary goes on to mention that strength is ***"the quality that allows someone to deal with problems in a determined and effective way."*** Studies have shown that strength can be influenced by race and/or sex; even the modern-day stereotypes play a factor into these perceptions. Stereotypes such as the "Angry Black Woman" or the "Independent Black Woman" tend to have black women harbor their feelings in order to avoid judgement. Which means showing any signs of hurt and/or expressing any form of weakness creates a complex with the "Strong Black Woman."   As "the strong one", no one seems to understand that there are times when you NEED someone to be there for you. Individuals never see that you are doing your best to keep a "strong" façade when you are either broken or breaking down deep inside. They feel that you can handle everything that comes your way with such a grace and a coolness as if nothing hurts you, breaks you down, makes you want to scream or "throw dem hands" (Yeah! I said it just like that!). People often assume that nothing makes you want to curse people out and spare NO feelings, makes you cry, keeps you up late at night asking God why or makes you second guess who you are and what God says you are! See, being "the strong one" has its good days, but its bad days happen more than anyone knows. What is really messed up is that on those tough days, you still have to be the "strong black woman" and "act" as if everything is okay. Let us go back to 2015 then fast

---

[2] http://www.mirriam-webster.com

forward to 2017; this is where I began to realize the new meaning of being "the strong one".

The 2015 Spring Semester at Guilford Technical Community College has just begun, and I am only five months away from being a college graduate. Picture this - everything is going well, and my grades are amazing. My teachers are impressed with my work ethic during my internships. Then suddenly, all of that drastically changes. Two weeks after my father's 80th birthday, I get a call from my brother telling me that our mother said that daddy did not look right. I rush home to find my father in the middle of having a stroke. Of course, I immediately sprang into action. Fast forward a few days later, Daddy is in ICU after having stint surgery and he is not the same. He is asking about his deceased family members and then he asks about Mommie's well-being. Nervously, I answer all his questions. Now, the doctors and nurses are saying that he must go to a nursing home for rehabilitation. At home, Mommie is concerned about her husband. She asks questions and I do my very best to answer all them. She tells me that she is trying to prepare herself for whatever God's will had in store. I did my best to smile and comfort her, when in actuality I am asking myself, "What did I do wrong? How could have I missed the signs again? He was fine when I left for school." About a week later, Daddy is being rushed back to the hospital again with another stroke, except this time, Hospice Palliative Care is called. The final report came in stating that they can only make him "comfortable." Wait! How did he go from sitting in my living room watching the game to his death bed? On April 16, 2015 my Daddy passes away.

Two years later, due to unfortunate events, Mommie is moved to a nursing home. At first glance, all was well - she was happy and thriving. She still missed Daddy, but her smile was getting bigger every day. She was able to get out of bed and was doing crafts with her neighbors. Then, just like Deja vu, there was a drastic change. Mommie begins to lose her appetite and does not want to get out of bed anymore. Having way more pain than usual, the nursing staff felt that it was best for her to go back to the hospital. The doctors told us that she had a huge ulcer on her lower back, that it was infected, and that it extended down to her spine. This news meant emergency surgery! We all prayed with Mommie; we prayed for a healing and speedy recovery, even in the midst of hearing her say that she was prepared to go home to be with her Heavenly Father (we were not ready for that). Things seemed to be getting better and Mommie started eating again. She had to stay in bed, but she was still smiling and praising God through it all. Months later, she stopped eating again, started sleeping a whole lot more and refused to take any medicine besides pain medicine (and that was given to her through the IV). Her nurses said the ulcer's infection was starting to return. Weeks later, just like with Daddy, Hospice Palliative Care was called in. They wanted to keep Mommie comfortable and want to help us prepare for the inevitable. On September 19, 2017 - two years, five months, three days and two hours later Mommie passes away.

"Aunt Nikki, you have to be the **strong one** because if you break, I do not know what I will do." I was identified as the "one" who had to hold it all together. I quickly had to become the "one" who had to continue to smile and be joyful, who could not cry and had to keep their feelings bottled inside. While others had their opportunity to be weak publicly, I became the "one" who could only fall apart, not even in private but only on the inside of my soul. For many of my family members, I am the "strong one" because I exude many of my Mommie's "strong" characteristics: caring, understanding, having a heart of gold, great listener, sympathetic and mild – tempered. My family sees me as reliable and dependable; to them, I am "the one" who can stand through any storm and stay focused when everything is going crazy. I am "the one" who keeps pushing no matter the circumstance; I am "the one" who encourages, inspires, and nurtures those who need it the most. What they do not know is that there were several nights where I could not sleep and could not bear to go home at the end of the day because of the pain that resided there. I was overwhelmed with regret and often asked myself what I could have done better; I even went to the extent of wishing that I had more time to make everything okay and to prove to my parents that I could be the best daughter ever.

Feelings of indescribable sadness would fall upon me at any given time. It would take me to dark places in my emotions and in my mental space; these "places" would have me wanting to end it all and just let it be over. All sorts of dark thoughts would flood my mind: "It is your fault that they are dead. You missed the signs once again. You are worthless. Nobody wants you here. Everyone hates you. Look how your Auntie hounded you, proving that you did not know what you were doing. Your husband deserves better. Your siblings deserve better. You know your brother was right, You ain't sh&$!'" I would sit and have all kinds of flashbacks of past suicidal attempts, one being of me wanting to take my dog outside for a walk with my bottle of prescribed pain pills in hand. I envisioned me sitting on the side of my apartment building, in the dark, and popping every pill that was in the bottle. I said to myself that I would just sit there in the dark, alone, and allow the pills to take me away. Another flashback had me standing on the curb of Yanceyville Street, praying for an eighteen-wheeler to come speeding down the road so I could walk out in front of it. My heart would flood with the feeling like, "No one understands what I am going through and quiet honestly, they do not care." I remember asking my husband, "What

130

does it feel like to have a nervous breakdown?" In total shock, he looked at me and said, "Honey, I do not know."

There were not enough words of comfort nor enough prayers that could have made me feel any better; "I'm so sorry for your loss" and "I'll be praying for you" became phrases that I despised. There were so many days that I just wanted to lay in the bed and cry, however, I resolved that since I had been labeled as the "Strong One" I had to be there for everyone else and make sure that all my responsibilities were handled. I must finish my courses. I must be a wife. I must be a sister. I must be an auntie. I must be whatever EVERYONE wants me to be.

It was not until I began reading this phenomenal book called, _The Shack_ by William P. Young, that my view as the "Strong One" began to change. The book talks about a man's spiritual encounter with God, Jesus, and the Holy Spirit. See, Eric's youngest daughter was kidnapped and killed by a serial children killer and Eric felt horrible. He accused himself for being a negligent father and interrogated himself about what he could have done differently. Eric even questioned God. So, one day out of the blue, Eric received a letter in his mailbox. The letter was from God asking Eric to come back to the shack (The shack is where police found Eric's daughter bloody dress). Eric went to the shack and during the encounter, God allows him to ask the questions that had been burning deep down inside. Eric asked God, "Why did you allow my little girl to be taken away? You say that You are everywhere, so where were you when my daughter needed you the most?" God, with a painful heart, told Eric that He was there with his daughter the whole time. God went on to say that, "Even though it may not look or feel like it I am there during the difficult times. I am even here for you, Eric. You do not have to go through this pain alone."

131

"I do not have to go through this pain alone! I DO NOT have to go through this ALONE!" Right there in those words, Jesus was reaching out to me. He found a beautiful way to penetrate my dark mind and mend my broken heart and spirit. My friend, at that very moment, I dropped the book and just began to cry uncontrollably. These were no longer tears of pain and regret but instead of joy and relief. Jesus showed me that I was NEVER alone because He was right there with me through the entire storm. He was there holding me and catching all the tears that I cried. Jesus removed the huge weight that was placed on my spirit and in my heart and had been the reason why I pressed to get my Associate's degree. He was the reason why I pressed to get my driver's license. He has been the reason why I did not lose my mind or commit suicide. He has been the reason why I could still smile and be joyful. He has been the reason why I can continue to raise my hands in worship and give Him His glory! The Bible clearly says that, **"the joy of the Lord is your strength," (*Nehemiah 8:10e*).**

In that very moment, an overwhelming "strength" began to flood my very soul. The "strength" that wanted to live to see another day, the wife that my husband deserves, the sister that my and the auntie that my nieces and nephews need; this word gave me the "strength" to be FREE! Kirk Franklin's song says it best:
"He intercedes for me. Protects me from things unseen. Right between God and me. He intercedes for me."

My friend, Jesus interceded for me. He became my STRENGTH when I was weak. He prayed the words that I could not and would not pray for myself. He stood in the gap and prevented my suicidal thoughts from becoming suicidal actions. It was **JESUS** the entire time! It was **JESUS** that everyone continued to see! I pray that you allow Jesus to intercede for you. I pray that you allow Him to be your STRENGTH in your times of weakness. I pray that you turn to

Him before turning to things that can harm you and/or destroy your family. Please know that no matter what, through Jesus Christ, **YOU are the "STRONG ONE!**

Brigitte Andrews

Brigitte was born and raised in Birmingham, AL where currently resides. She is a divorced mother of three very handsome grown men and has been employed in the court system for nearly twenty-five years! She grew up in surroundings that were not conducive for success but had a praying Granny who taught her how to use her imagination and dream BIG!! She realized at the age of nine that singing was her passion and in response to that passion, surrendered to this area of her calling by serving as a praise a worship leader at her local church. As a deeper response to this call, she is currently in the studio working on her very first EP! She is extremely excited and thankful to God for it!! One of her dreams is to finish her college education; this will become a reality for her next year! Brigitte believes that this is her moment and that through her continued submission to God, He will take her from glory to glory!

Brigitte's Dedication

I dedicate this project to my sons; Kevin, Jeremy and Daniel.

Kevin: I thank you for being so kind and thoughtful. You always inspire me to be better.

Jeremy: Thank you for being my lovable "Big Boy"! Through it all you've always been in my corner!

Daniel: Thank you for your " no sugar coating" advice! I always saw your heart and knew you only want me to soar!

Connect with Brigitte:

Phone: 205 203 5169
Email: bdandrews5@gmail.com
Queenchronicles5@gmail.com

CHAPTER 10
The Echo

Picking myself up off the floor and flopping on the twin bed, I now realized that what I feared the most has slapped me hard in the face! No more Sunday afternoons on the porch listening to the birds sing. No more playing 1-2-3 red light on the side of the house, homemade apple pies or fresh-squeezed lemonade or everything that I enjoyed. No more Granny - Granny's gone. I remember one school year that I needed an "overcoat" for the winter, Granny got her cane and we took the #8 bus downtown to buy my new coat from Piztiz Department Store. See, this was one of the best stores around and since black folk could now shop there, oh my goodness, it was a fun Saturday treat for me! My Granny's love for me was unshakeable! When I about ten years old, she wanted me to learn how to play the piano, so she talked to the church musician, Mrs. Saunderson to find out the cost and days that I would practice; Granny was really more excited about it than I was! That next Saturday morning, I took the #6 bus to Mrs. Saunderson's home, but my ten-year-old nerves got the best of me and I became so afraid that I did not get off that bus until I returned to my granny! As I was walking up the sidewalk, tears rolled down my face because I knew she would be so upset with me. She came to the front door, look at my little face, went back in the house and came out with her purse, coat and cane. My granny loved me!! She and I took the bus back to Mrs. Sauderson's house and Granny waited for me until my session was over. We then got back on the bus, went downtown and ate at our favorite cafeteria, Newberry's! Yes! My granny loved me!!

As time went on, Granny's and I relationship became stronger and stronger. I was her sweet baby and she was my example of how love walked in the earth. I chose to be like her, even when it came to loved ones that did not appreciate her. Earnest "Sam" Chapman, yep, that is my granddaddy. He came to live with granny on and off because he would not obey the rules of his woman's house! So, during the times when Ms. Claire would put him out, he would come to us. Granddaddy was a handsome and strong character. He worked many years for the railroad; in my presence he was a happy smiling man but there was pain in his heart that he masked with the bottles of gin and whiskey. You see about this time, he and my grandmother Bena had been divorced for years, which left my mother, her sister and her baby brother without a father in the home. As I think about it, maybe this is what I longed for; a father that would choose me, choose to take care of me and be my daddy. Well, let me move on for now. I would hear granddaddy knocking on the door and I would look at granny because I would be right under her in that big 'ole king size bed. She peered down at me from her glasses and said, "That's Sambo, go let 'em in." I had mixed feelings about that! On one hand, if he was not drunk, we would laugh and play for a while, but on the other hand if he was drunk, I would have to help him to the twin bed in the back hoping he made it to the bathroom. He smelled of tobacco and whiskey this time, so off to the back we went. I helped him get in bed, took off his shoes and before his head hit the pillow, he was snoring like a den of bears. This made granny furious, nevertheless she waited till morning to bless him out and boy did he get it! The next morning, we both woke up to bacon, eggs, grits and toast. Of course, granddaddy had his hot cup of coffee, black with sugar no cream. Granny let him eat and then she told him exactly how she felt.

What I loved about my granddaddy was that he never said a word back. He had much respect, but little appreciation because as soon as Ms. Claire was mad at him for being drunk and running around on her, he came back the same way. What I loved about my Granny was that she always let him in. The day before granny left me, granddaddy came by her home just to see her. He was not drunk nor had Ms. Claire put him out. He felt the need to see his mother and we had such a good time. My mother called granny to tell her that it was time for me to come home since I had school the next day. Reluctantly, I gathered my schoolbag and walked those five blocks home before it became dark. Granny was good, she was with Sambo and all was well. I guess sometime later, granddaddy went to his house and granny was left alone. I did not know this, because if I had known I would asked my mama to let me go back to my granny's house for the night but God knew I did not need to be there because He knew that it was time for Granny to come home. What I did not know was that Granny had had some heart trouble. She would have never told me that, so sometime during the night, Granny went to sleep and never woke up on this side of Heaven. She was alone in her big 'ole king size bed. I wonder if she was thinking of me, missing me as much as I missed her.

The next morning on my way to school, I had no clue when I knocked on the door that she was in Heaven. Coming back down that hill after school, changed my life! Now I had no refuge and no place of solace. I would have to endure the next years in fear, heartbreak and emotional assaults.

GRANNY'S GONE!

Granny's house was now occupied by her daughter and grandchildren, whom by the way, were not too fond of me. The only thing that was given to me after granny left, was her sewing machine; I never used it and never went back to that house again. This tragedy left me and my mama trying to find a way to heal. She found a way and so did I, but neither was a healing; it was another mechanism for more hurt to enter our lives. The next few months were very hard as I would walk past Granny's house knowing she was not there to give me a hug as I ran up the steps, no pot roast with potatoes, no sweet mama cornbread or vanilla ice cream for dessert waiting just for me; it was just a walk home alone with little joy of what was ahead of me. The absence of Granny closed the doors of expectation for good to ever show up in my life or so I believed but God had a plan.

Since Granny was now with Jesus and my mother was working, I had to become a "big girl". This meant coming straight home after school, doing my homework and making sure the house was clean. I really enjoyed being alone during those three hours. I had time to sing and dance while I did my chores. My mother was very clean and demanded that things be in order. I guess it came from her mother, Bena. What a remarkable woman Bena was!! Her eyesight was not that good from a child and one day, I think a Sunday, she was on the church bus and before she could have her seat the bus made a sudden stop. She hit the windshield so hard that the glass shattered with a lot of the glass scarring her pupils which left her completely blind, but she did not let that stop her! She went on to the school for the blind, then later went to Jefferson State Community College and finally graduating from the University of Alabama in Tuscaloosa with a bachelor's degree in Social Work!! She was amazing!! She later landed a job as a Social Worker/Counselor at the Bryce Mental Hospital in Tuscaloosa Alabama. I remember she would tell us the horror stories of her first few months. Some of them are laughable and others were frightening however, as time moved on her clients or patients grew to love, respect and protect her. What an amazing, strong, tenacious, courageous woman she was! Most of my memories of her was her humble beginnings. After divorcing Sambo, she moved into the Smithfield Housing Projects along with my uncle, Anthony, my aunt Leartis, her husband and my three cousins who lived three doors from MaDear (Bena). Oh, how I loved my Leartis and my cousins!! The days of chasing each other, playing in the sandbox and eating fudge pops were a wonderful antidote for the pain of Granny being gone. Christmas of 1979 brought all of that to a halt.

140

Leartis was murdered by her husband over a domestic dispute. The case was ruled "Involuntary Manslaughter" but we knew that it would eventually happen due to all the beatings Leartis endured for years. Oh, my Lord, another sweet soul whom I loved dearly was taken away from me again. He never served time and I never saw my cousins again, outside of an occasional summer when they would visit Madear and I just happened to be in Tuscaloosa at the time but it would never be the same; even to this day I have no real relationship with my first cousins. This make me very mad and sad. Mad? Yes, because Madear would try to blame my mother, Leartis' sister for her death. You see, when Madear left Birmingham to work in Tuscaloosa she told my mother to look out for Leartis. How could she to do that? Leartis was a grown woman and did not take kindly to my mother telling her what to do, besides, we lived in different parts of the city so when the Leartis was killed, a huge part of Madear was killed also. The part that remained was brutal toward my mother and me. I hated going to her home for the summer! It was not fun at all but a time of reading the dictionary and encyclopedia in order to help her with her patient's objective reports. Those three months was excruciating, but I ate good! The summers there were full of ridicule and humiliating remarks about my weight. I was not allowed to go outside because the "white folk" did not want me running around. When I returned home, it was not any better. I was told constantly that I was too fat or nobody like me, however there was one girl that became my friend. I would go downstairs at her grandmother's apartment and we would play with the dolls, color in the coloring books, watch television and eat fish sticks. Then one day, something happened to my friend. She was only about twelve years old, but the way she looked at me was different this time. The way she touched me was not fun. She was much bigger than me and the next thing I knew she was choking me, while touching me in my private area. She said that if I told anyone, she would kill me, and I believed it!

Honestly, most of my life has been filled with sexual assaults on me but somehow even going through it, God did not let it destroy me! Although I could have believed that I was now a lesbian, God did not allow those thoughts penetrate my mind!! Oh Lord, I thank you so much! I was finally able to break free from her grips because her grandmother died just a few months after the assault and there was no other of her relatives living in our apartment building or in the area. Thank you, Jesus! I remember I would cry out to the Lord even at the age of twelve, telling God how much I miss Granny and how much I loved Him! When Granny took me to church at the age of nine, so much of God has been deposited into my little spirit although I did not understand it. I soon learned that is why I enjoyed being alone, because I could talk to God when I looked in the sky, when I hear the birds sing or feeling the wind blow across my face. I heard God tell me how His love would make me strong and smart! I remember sitting on the steps on the playground at school with the little red Gideon's bible and just reading it. I had no idea what anything meant, but I knew I had to read it. That was the beginning of my love life with God. I did not know it at the time, but he was wooing me into his bosom. Now do not get it twisted - as I went into my teen years, I was very rebellious and "fast", always hoping to find a friend or a boyfriend. God heard my cry and sent my best friend, Carolyn.

We met in the fifth grade and to this day, we are BESTIES! Honey child, it was not easy, because every year after that we fought like cats and dogs, then about a week later we both were running to each other crying and apologizing for hurting the other. Isn't that crazy?! She's another sweet soul that I love dearly to this day.

THE COCOON

Although life began to feel a little more normal, I found myself in this place I called "The Cocoon". Let me explain. The outside world saw me as a smart, well-kept young lady but in my mind, I felt alone until one day when God spoke to me. It was after I had my first son, Kevin that God told me that He was going to make my life beautiful again. I did not understand the "again" part, so He explained it to me through the gifts He had placed in me. I found myself always wanting to help people, especially young ladies. It hurt me so bad to see a woman crying or sitting alone looking as though all hope was gone. Something in me, I should say, Holy Spirit, was always giving me words of encouragement to speak to women. Holy Spirit would always tell me that I was going to achieve more than I thought I could. Well, with my natural mind, I assume He was talking about a good job, nice home and a wonderful husband but none of those things truly satisfied me. I married and divorced, I lost my beautiful home and my job of fourteen years laid me off, so God was not talking about those "things. I learned that while I was in the cocoon, that my life was more than those things. Jesus was teaching me His way of thinking and doing! He was teaching me His character and how He moved in the earth.

I happened to be in the basement of my church one Sunday morning. Holy Spirit spoke to my heart, to the butterfly in the cocoon and the metamorphosis began! As I listened to the voice of Jesus, I soon learned that EVERYTHING I had gone through was not for me but instead, for you! I had to experience those trials, mistakes and even self-sabotage just to let you know that it is going to be alright. My relationship with God flourished and everyday knowing that He watched over me at night and He was smiling as I went about my day, made my heart long for His presence the more. One time I became so frustrated with life that I began to ask God a question, then

I hesitated and decided not to ask Him. Then with the most loving and profound voice, He said to me,

"Brigitte, I am NOT intimidated by your questions. Talk to me, if you want the answer in truth? Ask me".

That solidified my trust and confidence in my God to where now I take the pleasure in calling Him, DADDY! You see, I accepted the fact that my natural father did not have the capacity to love me or take care of me. He had the material means, but the cerebral strength was not there. My mother did not have the capacity to nurture or lead me to the place of high self-esteem, because it was never afforded to her. When I accepted all of that, I agreed with God that they did the best that knew to do. The cocoon began to tear, the cocoon began to open! I began to feel stronger and stronger; I broke out of the cocoon with one wing colored in purple, turquoise and gold and punched my way out. I used the other wing colored in purple, turquoise and gold pushing through the cocoon, breathing the wind of God's word and feeling the love of God lift me higher and higher into the sky! I am free! I choose not to let the echo of my past haunt me! I am free! I refuse to feel sad any more about Granny! She is cheering me on to every victory! I hear Granny now – "Go Baby Girl! I see you my baby girl!!" I understand that the cocoon was a prison. The cocoon was keeping me down or smothering me. The cocoon was protecting me, making sure all of my colors would be vibrant and fascinating with every move I made. The cocoon was my lullabies, my comfort, my salvation. The cocoon was God.

Sharon Benissan

Apostle Sharon Benissan was born on October 23, 1966 to Magnolia Cole and the Danny McCollum (deceased). She is the mother of two children, Ferreli Lamar McGilvary and Lavontraye Cornelius Andrews. Apostle Sharon Benissan married her amazing, wonderful, handsome and very anointed Apostle Cyriac Benissan on November 4. 2017. Apostle Sharon Benissan received the Lord Jesus Christ as her Savior in 1995 and her life has never been the same. In 1997, she did her initial sermon under the leadership of Bishop Mary Baldwin in Aberdeen, NC. and was ordained as elder in 2006 under the leadership of Dr. LD Reid in Raleigh, NC. God was preparing her for something she had not even imagined. In 2008-2010 Apostle Benissan was sent on assignment to pastor and serve the leaders of a ministry in St. Maarten, the Caribbean. While in the Caribbean, she served the ministry by bringing the leaders to a place where they could maintain the ministry in the absence of Senior Pastor Jennifer Brown (who was at the central location in London, England). Apostle Benissan attended the School of Prophets in 2011 and was certified by Dr. LD Reid. In 2012, she wrote a pamphlet entitled "Pulpit Incest-Things Kept Silent in the Church," and is currently working on "Married, Saved and Separated for His Glory". In 2013, she relocated to High Point, North Carolina where God gave her a desire and passion even more to help women from all lifestyles. Benissan has a strong desire to see women be all that God has called them to be. She began having meetings and prayer in her home where she invited women and began to pour out and into them. God placed a ministry of deliverance and birthing inside of her for women. In 2014, Women United in Prayer was birthed, and God used her in and out of the state to push and encourage women to be exactly what God has

Blessings + favor
Nikki
Apostle Shan

commissioned for them. In 2014, Benissan was certified as a Professional Life Coach specializing in Family, Business, Singles and College students and focusing on anyone that wants to get to that next level or place in life. In 2015 Apostle Sharon Benissan was ordained as Pastor/Founder of Global Impact Deliverance Ministries International by her spiritual parents, Apostle Charles & Deborah Bloom of Kingdom Minded Ministries International in Southern Pines, North Carolina. In 2016, she had the first Annual Women United in Prayer Conference where the lives of women were changed forever; it was in this meeting that she was able to empower women and help them understand the power of prayer. In 2018, Apostle Sharon Benissan along with her husband became the Overseers of The Blessed Gospel Church in Nairobi, Kenya where the Pastors are Rebecca and Thomas; Apostle Benissan also teaches bible study from time to time with connecting ministry in Pakistan via Skype. Apostle Benissan's favorite scripture is Philippians 1:6 where it states:

Being confident in this one thing, he that begun a good work in you shall perform it until the day of Jesus Christ.

The work the God started in you is completely in His hands and in His control; He is the only one that has the power to stop it so be confident in what He said and **FINISH THE WORK.**

Sharon's Dedication

To my Husband, Apostle Cyriac Benissan: I am so grateful that God have allowed me to meet such great man that I now call my husband. You have always supported me with anything I have ever wanted to do even if you did not agree with the timing. I have never had a moment with you that you have not pushed me to be the best that I can be both naturally and spiritually. It is awesome to have someone in life that will support you in all your endeavors and push you to the limit of your potential. I love and appreciate you for always encouraging me to write my story even when I did not feel like writing. I will forever be grateful for the support and love that I have in you.

To my motivation in life and my two first real loves, my children Ferreli Lamar McGilvary and Lavontraye Cornelius Andrews: I appreciate you for being the best children a mother could ever have. I love you and thank you so much for always supporting me and pushing me because you always saw me winning. I will be forever grateful to God for having such amazing children.

Connect with Sharon

Phone: (336) 491-0857

.info@globalimpactdmi.com

CHAPTER 11

My Teenage Reality

This road to writing about my life has been a very difficult one but I have conquered that fear and am so grateful to God for how He orchestrated things when I did not have a clue. I pray when you read about my story it will encourage you to keep going regardless of your situation or circumstance. I am motivated and more determined to help as many people as I can.

When I was younger, I always knew there was something that I had inside of me that was special. My grandmother raised me and always kept me in church. Proverbs 22:6 says:

"Train up a child in the way he should go and when he is old he will not depart from it."

I was tired of going to church all week long without a choice, but I was told I had to go. I went to church so much that I told myself "When I grow up, I am never going to church again." Of course, I did not know what I was saying at the time but as I got older, it all became clear to me. When I was a teenager, I wanted to do what other teenagers were doing and around that time I was sent to New York to be with my mother. I did not want to be with my mother because I did not know her like I knew my grandmother, but she always told me I needed to be with her because she was my mother. I remember when I went to New York I had a two-hour delay in Washington DC because I had to catch a bus from there to get to Long Island, New York. I arrived in New York and everything was different than what I was used to including my mother. When I got off the bus everyone was smiling, clapping their hands and saying how pretty I and my hair was (which very long). I did not know how to feel. I was only eleven years old and did not know these people that I was around and did not know this place. I still did not want to be on Long Island, but I had no choice, so I decided to make the best of it. When I got to my mom's house, I saw my sister that I was meeting for the first time; I truly did not know how to feel about any of it. I remember being angry and saying to myself, "who is this and where did she come from?" I need you to understand I was around eleven years old and it was just me all that time so getting to know my mother as well as meeting my sister at the same time was too much for me. I remember my mother getting ready for work and even having things to do and being left with my sister. I was mean to my sister just because of the attention she was getting from my mother that I would never get. I was mad most of the time. I remember calling my mother "Mom" and her response being silence; this pushed me away even more. I remember asking my mother, "did you hear me," and she would answer, "yes"; this left me confused and filled with questions as to why my mother did not want me to call her mom. I started staying at the park longer during the day and just trying to find something to keep me busy, so I did not have to be at home.

So finally, I had a chance to meet some of my mother's friends as well as their children. It was great to see some children my age and I began to hang out with them, but little did I know that they were into all the wrong things. During that summer I discovered that one of the boys liked me and I guess I liked him too so we started talking more and hanging out more as a group but that did not keep me from getting closer to him. When it was time for me to go back home, I did not want to go because I was getting used to being around my mother and sister and I was excited about the friends that I had made.

I would go to Long Island every year until it was time for me to graduate high school. When I was fourteen years old, I started hanging out with a group of people that were friends with the friends I already had, and they introduced me to drugs. They took me to this home where all of this "stuff" was set up like a lab and explained to me what was going on. They showed me the whole process of how to make crack cocaine and how to split up or cut it up before distribution and sales. All of this was really mind blowing to me but interesting all at the same time; the more I hung out with them the more I wanted to do what they were doing. My mother had no idea what I was into and I noticed when they were around my mother, they would be so nice but different when out of her presence and she never saw through it. I started going to the park at different times with them and saw actual transactions of how to make sales on the streets. They took me back to the house where the cooking, cutting and packaging were taking place; there was also another room in the house that only certain people could go into. The guy that was over the whole operation took me into this room to have a conversation with me to see if I was in and assumed I was in because I was there. The one thing that caught my attention more than anything was all the money I saw and the assignment to keep up with every dollar that came in. I was shocked and scared at the same time, but he never knew it and when he told me how much money I could make just doing what he asked me to do I was definitely in. I had already told my mother that I wanted to get a job and so here was the opportunity that I was looking for or so I thought. I would call myself going to the park to hang out with friends and that ended in a fight or shoot out; yes, they gave me a gun and I was scared out of my mind, but I was too far in and would not turn around because they told me they would always have my back no matter what. I dd not know that I was participating in gang activity until we were confronted by a group of people wearing white tee shirts and jeans, but they all had on the same baseball cap. They told us that we were in the wrong area and we needed to leave and of course we rebelled; a fight broke out and we ended up

151

fighting and shooting. This was one of the scariest things I had experienced by far. We made it out of that without anyone being killed or hurt; when we got back to the house the person that was over us said, "Great job! If you ever need me I will be right here for each of you; job well done tonight!"

I went home and my mother did not have a clue what I had been through. I remember that cold and scary feeling that I had because I had shot a gun for the very first time; I did not know what I was doing but following my friends. A few weeks later, I was hanging out with this group of friends again and we got rushed by another group of people outside of this little Jamaican joint about three or four block from where the main house was as we were just chilling trying to get something to eat. This time we played it cool and when we got back to the house, the person that was the leader began to tell us what was going down later that week. We went to what appeared to be a celebration at the park that ended up being an actual shoot out again but this time I heard the bullets as they were going by my face. I started to run, but this time, I ran all the way to my mother's house and got in the bed. I started thinking about what just happened and how I could have lost my life or taken someone else's life. This thing really hit home for me and caused me to leave the drugs and money alone. I kept dealing with the drugs because I had enough money to pay cash for a car and being a fifteen-year-old who wanted to work, that was crazy to me. Of course, I did not understand it all but when I tell you we serve an amazing God because even when I was hanging out with the wrong crowd God covered me; even when I was not thinking about anything but myself, He still covered me.

I wanted to tell my testimony about what happened to me as a teenager because even when I could not take care of or watch over myself God was always there for me and I still did not want to serve Him because I felt that I was

152

too young and had so much life ahead of me. Although my grandmother had kept me in church all that time, I still did not think about that because I was tired of going to church as well. I eventually came back to North Carolina and by that time it was a wrap because if I had stayed on Long Island, New York my life would have taken another wrong turn; I would have probably been locked up, still on the streets or dead.

I want people to know that you can come out of anything even if it is something that happened to you a long time ago or when you were younger God is able to change your whole life. I have to say that my grandmother put something inside of me that stayed with me even when I did not want to have anything else to do with church at all. The seed was planted because she did not ask me, but instead made me, and lived the life that she was talking about in front of me. She never said one thing and lived another. My grandmother told me about God and the things that He could do for me. I did not always understand but I believed everything she said to me. When she talked about God, at times I did not want to listen because that is all she talked about, but I am grateful that she was persistent and consistent. I do not even want to imagine where I would be if she did not introduce me to this supernatural being called God.

I want you to know that God had His hand of love covering my life at the young age of fifteen. I thought what I was introduced to in New York was something big until I learned later that it was only taking me to an early grave or in somebody's jail.

Being confident in this one thing he that has begun a good work in you is able to perform it until the day of Jesus Christ.

-Philippians 1:6

"For I know the thoughts that I think toward you saith the Lord, thoughts of peace and not of evil, to give you an expected end." This mean not only will he showed us with success and blessings but there is also a purpose for suffering.

-Jeremiah 29:11

"Greater love hath no man than this, that a man lay down his life for his friends." Jesus will stick closer to you than a friend so when you feel you are all alone just know that you have a friend in Jesus.

-John 15:13

"Be strong and courageous, do not be afraid or terrified because of them for the Lord your God goes with you, He will never leave you nor forsake you."

- Deuteronomy 31:6

As I was going through all the things I endured in New York, some people were saying good things as well as bad. When I began to understand who God really was in my life, clarity set in and I focused on the power of encouragement. The words we speak have power and its either positive or negative power. You already know how powerful words are. We can use our words to bring joy or sorrow, healing or hurt, discouragement or encouragement. The book of Proverbs says that words are like a hammer, a fire, a cup of cold water on a hot day. Have you ever known someone that believed in you and let you know it by frequently speaking words of encouragement and praise? This is the kind of person who made you believe in yourself, in your future, and that you could do whatever it takes to get there. These are the kind of people you need in your life.

"Death and life are in the power of the tongue, and those who love it and indulge it will eat its fruit and bear the consequences of their words".
-Proverbs 18:21

"The mouth of the righteous is a fountain of life and his words of wisdom are a source of blessing, but the mouth of the wicked conceals violence and evil".   -
Proverbs 10:11

"Wise men store up and treasure knowledge (in mind and heart) but with the mouth of the foolish, ruin is at hand."

-Proverbs 10:14

"Let us therefore follow after the things which make for peace, and things where with one may edify another."

-Romans 14:19

"Wherefore comfort and encourage yourselves together, and edify one another, even as also ye do."
-1

Thessalonians 5:11

"Take heed, brethren, lest there be in any of you an evil heart of unbelief, in departing from the living God."
-Hebrews 3:12

"But exhort one another daily, while it is called today; lest any of you be hardened through the deceitfulness of sin."
-Hebrews 3:13

"And let us consider one another to provoke unto love and to good works."   **— Hebrews 10:24**

"Not forsaking the assembling of ourselves together, as the manner of some is; but exhorting one another: and so much the more, as ye see the day approaching."

-Hebrews 10:25

Queena McKee Clyburn

Queena McKee Clyburn was born in Greensboro, N.C. She is a master hairstylist she has been in the beauty industry for over twenty years. Her motto for life is to help people look like where they are going to and not what they are going through. She is a lifetime entrepreneur at heart, Paparazzi Accessories, Mary Kay Cosmetics and Clyburn Catering just to name a few. She is being featured in several magazines and has also managed and owned several successful salons. In 2012, she married Stewart Clyburn, the love of her life. She was licensed and ordained as a minister in January 2016 and is currently being elevated in ministry to Pastor at Ignited Blue Apostolic Church. Evangelism is her Passion and her optimism and determination makes her amazing in family, love and ministry.

Queena's Dedication

To the four most influential people in my life:
My Husband Stewart Clyburn the love of my life: You truly teach me what love and understanding are about. You love and accept me for who I am there is nothing more special to me.

My mentor and leader, Apostle Alicia Foust. Thank you for Believing and pushing me.

My Mother, Alice Wise. Thank you for teaching me to never give up, the power of endurance and the legacy of entrepreneurship.

To my Lord and Savior Jesus Christ: Thank You for giving your life for mine!

Connect with Queena

Phone: 336-512-1774
Email: queenaclyburn@gmail.com

https://www.marykay.com/QMcKeeClyburn

https://queensclassyhair.mayvenn.com/

Bit.ly/ThePaparazziQueen

CHAPTER 12
From Rejected to Elected

When most of us look at our calendars, especially after August, we begin to count down to the holidays; time is something I have never quite gotten the concept of. As a little girl whose mother worked third shift, my nights were my days in my days were my nights. I spent a lot of time lying awake waiting for her. The anticipation of her arrival would wake me early in the morning. The truth is, I am still that way until this very day. It is amazing how the most simple things can shape and mold your life. As a child, I never quite fit in and was not a typical child because I grew in the house with my mom and my grandmother. I hung around with my great-grandmother, grandmother, mom and my aunt; these are of the strongest women I have ever met.

I was the only child in my family in my city until the age of nine years old. I watched them endure heartache and deal with bills and everyday life. I watched them go through relationships and deal with other people which was what molded and shaped me for my life. As a result, I became the little girl who was always in "grown folk's business"; you know that thing where most children dismissed themselves from the room. At that age, of course, I was too small to be in grown folk's business, but in my mind I think "these kids around here don't have any business," even though we were all the same age. This will become what I would consider my normal - always being in the middle.

As a little girl I can recall going to the park and seeing a little girl play with her father. "Push me Daddy!", she said, and he did. I sat on the far end of the swing and watched them for a little while. The swing kept going higher and higher. They were still there but I was so focused on kicking my feet until it was going fast enough, and I no longer had to. I stopped watching them, and before I knew it, found myself soaring high. This was one of the first times

I realized that my father was not in my life and it was just going to have to be ok. I was just going to have to buckle down, kick my feet, be a big girl and fly. This taught me a valuable lesson that I could do anything, and I did not need a man to do it for me. I tried so hard not to be jealous but as I grew, on the inside, some days my daddy was all I wanted.

The absence of my father was a touchy subject in the house because most men I saw were always doing something wrong (and remember I was always listening to what was going on in the adult world – you know, the grown folk's business.) At the time I did not realize that this was molding me and would affect the way I saw men, their worth and the position they were to play in my life. I did not recognize any of this was wrong; for me, my daddy not being there was normal along with the absence of men in my immediate family. I made up in my mind as a little girl that all they did was lie and cheat and that I did not need a man to be successful. I learned all of this while listening to "grown folk's business." In that moment, I learned I could do anything I put my mind to, but something changed when I started becoming a teenager.

I was a regular kid full of energy hope and ready for anything but just a little on the chunky side. You know, kids can be pretty mean, especially when those things called words start flying like bullets. They would say to me, "you better stop eating all that food! You're gonna to be fat! You're gonna be big as a house!' The insults continued with, "you don't need to give her everything she wants to eat. She needs to go on a diet! Go outside and run around." It seemed as if someone always had something to say about me. I would often say to myself, "They are talking about me, but they need to look in the mirror." I kept trying not to hear them or let their words hurt me, but it did not work. The things I disliked the most become my two new best friends, boys and food, because they do not judge me. All the boys said, "she's cute for a big girl." Sometimes, people do not realize how their words mold and hurt people at the same time; the way I saw it, their words came out fully loaded and were prepared for a mass murder. These words came for my very life, murdering my self-esteem, my self-image and my self-worth. This attack seemed to push me right to the thing they said I did not need but they were both there to receive me with open arms.

As I walked in the shadow of their words something began to happen. You might call it destiny or fate, but I began to see myself, and to be honest, I have no idea what I saw. I become a young lady, cute in the face and thick in the waste. Now, no longer a victim, I was the victimizer and learned how to use my words to manipulate others and to get anything I wanted. Remember words have power: they can shape and tear down too but can also encourage and empower. I got to the place where I would no longer let people speak to me; I was determined that I was going to be the one who was speaking. You see, I felt like I spent all my life listening to people and "their words,"; as I grew up, I began to use those words that they said to me against them or at least that is what I thought. I became a master manipulator cutting down and taking advantage of anyone who was in my path. You see friendly fire is the worst when you hurt someone who is innocent. Many people try to love me along but the way I always seem to get what I wanted from them and disappear. It was easier that way - no connections and no responsibility and simply reducing it to instant gratification. I did not realize what I was doing to myself or the people around me; it was around that time that I discover this thing called sex and that, along with my word "game" was like a perfectly mixed cocktail for destruction. I put myself in several situations where I could have gotten killed while in hotel rooms with strangers wild and crazy parties with friends and at times, I cannot believe

I made it out of out of that. Even when I was in those situations, people would always say there was something different about me; they would tell me things like "You're special. You're so nice." I thought I was faking all of it and never realized that it was a part of my DNA. I was not a mean girl; I was always nice and polite. You would never know some of the thoughts I had in the back of mind.

I grew in wisdom and realized that hurt people hurt people; that lifestyle quickly grew old. During all of this time, as I was accomplishing goals and moving forward in life, I graduated from high school. In spite of being diagnosed with dyslexia (which means I have trouble reading and writing), I have always been a girl for words and went on to receive a degree in cosmetology. Thankfully I always had great teachers to help me.

So it is time to fast forward: at this point I was on top of the world I really thought I had everything I needed; I had a car, a place to stay and no kids to hold me back. I was an independent woman. In my mind I really thought I had a going on but quickly, all the things I did not have became my desire. The feelings of challenge stood and looked at me face to face: I had hurt so many and left so many skeletons along the way and had no idea how I would begin to reshape my life and fix the broken parts of it all. You see, I could blame all of this on the words that people spoke over me in the beginning, but I cannot because as an adults, we must take responsibility and accountability for every word that we speak over ourselves. I returned to my roots: you see my great-grandmother used to take me to church every Sunday when I was a little girl and I did not realize what those words I heard were doing for my life. The Bible says:

"Train up a child in the way that they should go and when he is old, he will not depart from it." – Proverbs 22:6 (KJV)

I went away for season but as I grew, I knew exactly where to return home - church. Like anyone else who joins the church, you go through a season where you have one foot in the door of the church and one in the world, but when you see these words were different you begin to pursue the door of life. It was in this atmosphere that I found the words of joy, peace, kindness and encouragement and as I continued to hear these words over and over again, I began to become better! I began to love myself and love people. God looked beyond my faults and saw exactly what I needed. My mind was renewed my life was changed. I gave my life to Jesus but there was still something missing.

I never had people who spoke, not to the person I was, but to who they saw me becoming. To make a long story short, I met amazing man when I was in the world. I truly took him for granted but he was my friend. He was one of the first people to tell me that they loved me, and I believed they meant it. In my life I had a bad habit; in hindsight I called it protecting myself from people who "loved me." When someone showed me that they were a good person and truly cared about me, I would run, because I had yet to discover how to love myself and had come to the conclusion that since I could not love me there was no way that anyone else could. I would avoid all contact if I had to because of this lie that I had accepted as my truth.

Despite this battle, this amazing man kept showing up in my life; it just so happened that circumstance and purpose came together and now I am his wife. Sometimes I cannot believe that I went through what I went through but what I want you to know is that you cannot change what people think about you or say about you but instead, you have the power to make a decision to change your mind. You must allow God to renew your mind. You must begin to think about who the person God saw when He spoke the

163

words of destiny and purpose concerning you. Take this moment, even as your read, to realize that many may have said things to hurt you but had no idea who they were talking to. You see, what I found out was that even though the words came, the word of God can change anything that anyone has ever spoken over you. God will renew your mind and change your life; you have power to speak blessings and overflow over yourself. The only words that matter are the ones that come from God our Father. This changed my life: Words have taken my world from the fat fatherless fast little girl who is promiscuous and looking for love to a faithful, friendly forgiving, free wife and Pastor of the Gospel of Jesus Christ. God has no respect of person and if He can do all of this for me just imagine what He is going to do for you.

Rose Hall

Rose Hall is a Resourceful, Outgoing, Servant-leading Entrepreneur Motivating Helper of ALL. She is a faithful wife, loving mother of four, a Registered Nurse and Health Solutions Expert. She is currently the publisher of the digital newspaper, "Daily Wellness Lifestyle News." She is one of the Best-Selling Co-Authors in the 3 books, It Takes Money Honey, Women of Purpose 365-day Devotional and Daily Dose of Declarations. She loves God, writing poetry, and encouraging others to GROW to their maximum potential.

Rose's Dedication

I dedicate this book to my Lord and Savior Jesus Christ and my children: KNOW that WITH GOD ALL THINGS ARE POSSIBLE! He will never Leave you nor Forsake you so TRUST GOD! He is the Author and Finisher of your Faith!

Connect with Rose

Phone#: 336-602-4819

Email: askrosehall@gmail.com
Website: www.about.me/rosemhall
Facebook: Destinations4u - Rose Hall
Instagram: www.instagram.com/ubhealthe2

.

CHAPTER 13

AGAINST ALL ODDS

I AM ROSE and my purpose is to **R**estore **O**thers **S**erve and **E**mpower but it did not start out that way. You see, I was born in Newark, New Jersey to a single young lady at the age of nineteen who was involved with an older man. This older man was my father; we never met. He was about twenty-five years older than my mother whom I cannot remember. I cannot remember my biological parents because, as I was told, they argued a lot. One day, they had a heated argument, so my father took me at the age of six months old from my mother to his good friend's house and told them not to let my mother get me. He said that he would return but that never happened. I was abandoned.

An innocent child abandoned by her parents living without a care in the world; this is how I ended up being cared for and loved by Mr. and Mrs. Barney and their six children who added me as number seven. Growing up with this family, we had some fun-loving times but there were also some challenges. Some things I may have forgotten but some I will never forget. I remember when I was a little girl being rescued by a firefighter who was wearing a mask. He woke me up out of my bed and covered me with a blanket because my siblings forgot I was inside while my mom was at work when our home caught on fire. I almost died. I remember when I was a little girl going to the beach in New Jersey with my cousins and was swimming underwater with my eyes closed. When I came up for air, I sank down to what felt like a bottomless pit and popped back up and yelling, "Help! Help!" I could see my family from a distance while spitting water and my hands reaching up when all of a sudden, I was rescued again by the lifeguard on duty and he was the one who brought me to shore. I also remember being a little girl at age five years old: I was so eager to start school that one day I woke up, got dressed and walked myself to school while my family was home asleep. Little did I know, my mom had not registered me for school yet, but I was smart enough to tell the Principal how to drive me safely home. I almost died. I was rescued and protected!

As a baby, I was initially in a two-parent home because Mr. Barney and my dad were good friends. Growing up as a child, him and his wife, who I call "my mom" separated. She raised me in a single-parent home with my older siblings who later had children of their own. We lived in nice decent homes, although we lived in the projects for a little while with my grandparents (at least it felt that way.) I was at their home a lot until I was about eight years old; this was when I finally entered elementary school. I recall being tested out and skipping kindergarten and second grade. My grandmother was the first one to tell me that "my mom" was not my real mother at that time too. She told me before my mom even got a chance to tell me. It was at this time that I believe I started having what they now call "night terrors."; these horrific events are like nightmares but far more dramatic. I could hear voices of the evil one and I feared his darkness.

Speaking of darkness, I remember a dark time in my life as a little girl while living in my grandmother's home. I was being treated for urinary tract infections repeatedly because I held my urine a lot to avoid the burning sensation in my vaginal area due to my so-called cousin from the South sexually molesting me with his fingers. He was an older teenager and I was less than nine years old; he would threaten to hurt me and even kill me if I ever told anyone. I would repeatedly lie to my mom by saying I had fallen and hurt myself to explain why I hurt "down there." At the age of seven, my birth mom died but I was not officially adopted, and my last name changed until I was nine years old and in the fourth grade. It was not soon after this time that history tried to repeat itself. When I was about ten years old, a man who lived in the same building as my mom

168

and I would flirt with me and my friends. He would show us his large fingers and talked about touching us with them. This time I told my mom and the rest is history. I was molested. I was a liar. I was adopted.

During my preteen years I had so many hormone changes that I can only recall one good year and that was at age twelve when I met my biological grandparents and great grandparents, my aunt, three uncles, cousins and most of all, my oldest biological brother. I remember this day like it was yesterday when they came to our home and knocked on the front door! I was oh so happy! It was during this same year that I found out that my biological father died in his 50's and my mother at age 26. I had also found out that I have about four more biological siblings from my mother that I have never met, even until this day. My mom would allow me to go to over my biological grandmother's home sometimes as well; I am still connected to my original family today. I was restored.

How about those teenage years? If you ask me, I thought my teenager years were the worst years of my life! I must say at least I felt that way at the time, but now I understand it was for my good. You see, my mom was strict on me. I had to come in the house when the streetlights came on. If I was outside playing with my friends and some boys came near my porch, I had to go back in the house until they left. I remember my mom punished me one time for a week in the summertime but by time she had finished adding a week for every little thing, I was on punishment for the entire summer!

There were also some disappointments and not so proud moments in my life that now I know, was not only a part of my process, but my life journey. One time I ran away when I was supposed to be going to the grocery store for my mom; I lied and said I was kidnapped. I had my family and everyone in my neighborhood looking for me. Today I can say I also survived an abortion when I was sixteen years old. This was a family secret for years that only my mom and the cousin who took me to the abortion clinic knew about at that time. This may come as a shock to many as you are reading my story. Growing up in the inner cities of North Jersey I was exposed to all kinds of verbal, emotional, physical, and drug abuse and even had the spirit of addiction living among some of my family members. I was a liar. I was a killer.

Would you believe that through all of this, I have never lost my mind, hopes and dreams to grow-up and go off to college and one day to become somebody in this world while being able to make a difference by touching the lives of others? During my school days every year I remained an Honor Roll student and have received many Academic Achievement Awards. I graduated from High School with a 4.0 at the top 10% of my graduating class. I was the first person out of my adoptive siblings to graduate high school, go off to college, and to give my life to Jesus Christ and willingly serve Him with my whole heart at the ripe age of twenty-four. Since this new birth, God has blessed me to have a husband and I've been married for almost nineteen years now! He has blessed the fruit of my womb, despite my past, to be able to birth four beautiful children in this world with one being a set of twin girls! There is NOTHING my God cannot do! What He make happen for others He'll do the same for YOU!   As I reflect over my life, I do not recall having parental support while I was away in college. My adopted mom's dream was for me to graduate high school, so she uprooted me at age seventeen while in my junior year from New Jersey to North Carolina to make sure I graduated, in which I did at age eighteen. Since I was considered independent at that age, if college was to be then it was up to me! I will forever be grateful for all my teachers and guidance counselors who took their time out to help me to become the person I AM today. We may not have agreed on some things, but they were like guardian angels to me. I remember when my senior year guidance counselor took me to my freshmen orientation. I also had a great high school friend who I met here in North Carolina that helped me to get to college and move into my dorm room. All in all, I graduated from college with over a 3.0 GPA with a B.S. in Foods and Nutrition on a full scholarship. I later became a Registered Dietitian and licensed by the state. Hallelujah! Thank You Jesus!!

After receiving my first degree, three years later I was able to marry my best friend at age twenty-seven and God blessed us with a honeymoon baby. I later went back to college when I was thirty years old to start Nursing School. I initially started at a community college and had to repeat a nursing course one time but did not let that stop me. Right before starting my last quarter, and before graduating at the community level, I got accepted to an Accelerated Nursing program at the university. It was an all-expense paid program with a $500 monthly stipend and a minimum of three years job commitment attached to it! I stepped out on faith and I graduated with High Honors receiving a four-year BSN degree in 13 months! To God be ALL the Glory!!!

By the grace of God after receiving my two bachelor's degrees, God blessed my husband and I with three more children. An older girl at age thirty-five and last two children were beautiful twin girls at age forty after having a miscarriage; I say He gave us double for our trouble. During this pregnancy Twin A's heartbeat had dropped down into the 70's, so my primary doctor rushed me to see the heart doctor (Cardiologist) who then looked and said, "Twin A's heartbeat is normal," and then decided to look at Twin B. To make a long story short, they then diagnosed Twin B with a congenital heart defect. The doctors did not think she would survive the pregnancy, but we believed the report of the Lord!

Only my prayer partners including my husband knew what was going on; I was determined to walk by faith and not by sight (2 Corinthians 5:7- NKJV). I went to the Cardiologist weekly while working my full-time job as a Hospice Case Manager up until I was 33 weeks pregnant. When the medical team realized that we survived the pregnancy, they came up with a plan to quickly transport Twin B to another hospital immediately after the delivery, to have heart surgery to repair her tricuspid valve. Little did they know that on the delivery day at thirty-seven weeks, when they took her from me to do the heart surgery, the GREAT PHYSICIAN had already healed her, and no physical surgery was needed from man! Hallelujah! Thank you, Jesus! GOD is Good!

Be STILL and KNOW that HE is GOD (Psalm 46:10-KJV). You see although, I was born out of wedlock, abandoned as a baby, raised in a single-parent home, almost died by fire and by water, a victim of molestation, a runaway, a liar, killer, and in all honesty at one point a thief, I was still able to receive the gift of salvation from my sins through faith in the Lord Jesus Christ. As it is written, all have sinned and come short of His Glory (Romans 3:23-KJV). There is none righteous, no not one (Romans 3:10-KJV). Though my father and mother forsake (abandon) me, the Lord will receive me (Psalm 27:10-NIV). Today I AM washed in His blood, sanctified, and justified in the name of the Lord Jesus Christ and in the Spirit of God (1 Corinthians 6:11-NKJV). I AM delivered and set free because he has removed my sins as far as the east is from the west (Psalm 103:12-NIV)

As for the devil, he intended to harm me, but God intended it all for good, in order to accomplish what is now being done, the saving of many lives. (Genesis 50:20-NIV). Today I can say by the Grace of God, I AM a high school graduate, a two- times college graduate with two Bachelor's Degrees, a Licensed Registered Dietitian, a

Registered Nurse, an Entrepreneur, and a three - times #1 Amazon Best-Selling Author to God Be All the Glory!! I am a proud wife, a loving mother of four but most of all I AM proud to be WHO GOD SAID I AM! I AM an Overcomer and KNOW that you are an OVERCOMER too! AGAINST ALL ODDS!

Rolonda Hernandez

Poet, Author, Advocate are just a few of the many hats that Rolonda Hernandez wears.

From her passionate development of civic engagement programs like, *Opportunity Homes*, which promotes homeownership and financial literacy among single mothers to her activism in founding *The Cannady Project*, which empowers formally-incarcerated individuals with the acumen to establish themselves as entrepreneurs, Rolonda has committed her life's work to the betterment of her community, and the uplift of all "her people".

Always grateful for the foundation of education, spirituality, and social-activism she received in her hometown of Raleigh, N.C., Hernandez has always used her exposure to a myriad of cultures, and life-perspectives to fuel her mission of self-mastery through service. Her expertise as a Virtual Chief Operating Officer has been lauded by her peers.

Having to overcome obstacles on her journey as a single-mother, a woman of color in a male-dominated field of work, and with an unconventional approach to education, Rolonda has used her personal challenges, and her professional prowess, to elevate the lives of herself and those in her community that society has dismissed, and discarded.

Writer, Mother, Activist, Leader, Entrepreneur, Visionary. Rolonda Hernandez is an emerging voice of "her people", with a passion to lead her community through a true socio-economic Exodus.

Rolonda's Dedication

Dedicated to the Most High Yah! This is my promise.

Connect with Rolanda

Download your chapter workbook at:
www.iamrolonda.com
Linkedin: www.linkedin.com/in/rolonda
Instagram: rolondathestrategist

CHAPTER 14

Statistically Speaking

BOOM. BOOM. BOOM.
"It's the police department! Open up with your hands up!
shuffle, muffle Get on the ground NOW!"
"Wait, don't shoot! I am down! My wife is only person in
the house. She pregnant. Please don't shoot her. Look, I'm
down." The sound of the shuffling of multiple feet covered
with combat boots filled the atmosphere. "Police
department! Come out with your hands up!" "I am in here.
Please don't shoot. MY HANDS UP!!" Looking down a barrel
of an officer's gun that is so close to my face I can feel the
coolness of the winter's morning frost off the officer's
weapon. **thinking** How in the world did I get here!
****

See like many others, I am not supposed to be here.
Sharing my life's journey. I should have been in a mental
facility ward multiple times over, but Yah! Yah has been the
guiding force through all that I have been and who I am
becoming. America has this dream that feeds us as a
guiding principle of where we are supposed to aspire to –
reach towards. I say the dream is a nightmare for
individuals like me who hate boxes. I live life to be able to
love freely. I have seen love do many things – beautiful and
strange. Love can inspire or be someone's detriment if used
incorrectly; maybe that is how I got in that place with the
officer's gun in my face that morning.

How can love place me in the face of a weapon?
Easy. Dealing with environments because of an individual
you love, can have your life turned upside down in a
second. I could have been a Kemba Smith. She was
sentenced to 24.5 years in prison for conspiracy to
participate in her boyfriend's drug activities, a non-violent,

first-time offense.[3] Lives turned around in a minute because of that wonderful thing we seek. Hindsight is always 20/20.

I was not raised in an environment that was conducive to this type of behavior. I came from a middle-class Southern Baptist family home created by high school sweethearts, which are still married to this day. My father and mother consistently broke records in their professional and private lives. Through the numerous youth community groups, we were taught to help and try to reach all people and give back to anyone in need. As a high schooler that supported her family while they pursued their entrepreneurial spirits, I worked three jobs to get the things I wanted. I took college level courses within my high school curriculum to top it off. I was always doing something to uplift my fellow man; the spirit of excellence was drilled in me since I can remember. Your good, can always be your better. I was going somewhere with my future bright with high plans of being a doctor in a prestige HBCU teaching African American Studies in tow.

My dissertation was all ready to go before I got my acceptance letter from the colleges. I was ready for this thing called "adulting." So, you can imagine where my mind was when I found out I was a part of the 33% that was pregnant at the age of seventeen. Yes, that top scholar student did not calculate the famous demise of many people for centuries – love.

My senior year probably was so confusing to someone from the outside looking in. Here you have a well-versed promising teenager before the school fall break, who turns into a broken-spirited teen that is just trying to graduate. Thank goodness for my child's father. He tried his best to make the right decisions for his new budding family by paying for me to get back and forth from school. We

---

[3] (https://www.sentencingproject.org/issues/women/)

decided collectively that above all else, we were going to graduate - no dropouts. He came from the other side of the tracks as the elders would say. The kryptonite of a 'good girl'. He was used to the teenage pregnancies and governmental programs, unlike myself. I had never seen what that world looked like before that moment. I was led to believe there was no assistance for a teenager that was pregnant and still in school. My mind took me thinking from about what items I needed to lace my dorm room with to me begging for help to survive. The pressures of survival, graduation and a 180-degree change of my environment sent me into an unknowingly depression. I did not have the tools to understand what depression was, but I knew the old me was gone just that quick.

My new future looked bleak. Looking at my surroundings of poverty, that I have only seen in afterschool specials and Lifetime movies, this was all new to me. I had no parents, no family to call on and my friends had gone off to college like we all planned and talked about all of these years. Chaos, fights, guns and drugs were my new life now. I used to catch myself saying, "Is this life now? Is this my future - to strive to have children so your rent allocation can go up for your house or your food stamps count can go up on your next renewal?" I learned quickly those that live this life do not make it, instead either end up locked up, wasting space by achieving nothing or six feet under. I knew I had more potential than this world was showing. On the other hand, the love of my life became controlling and then abusive. I was lost and alone. During that duration of my pregnancies, I was dumped into a world of "by any means necessary," do or die, you know — survival of the fittest. I had to do what I had to do to make sure my babies did not have to go down this tremulous journey. When you can go a whole year without breaking a smile or laugh — the flame of hope one holds seems to dim quickly. The journey got so tough and dim, I found myself contemplating suicide. Earlier or later, I realized, I had created a cycle to help someone

179

else become their greatest even if that meant sacrificing myself.

Now that I had a child, I did not want him to be another little black boy lost. He was my inspiration to breathe every second that became the hour to complete the day as the walking dead, or "dead from the head" down as I called it. Motivation in that type of environment is a rarity. If I was going to do this, I loved him enough to take him too. It took a moment of revelation to realize if I cannot live for myself, I will live for my son (Sun). He did not ask to be here; however, he shall have the opportunities his father and I stripped away from our youth. If it is one thing, I am a woman of my word. My word is my bond. Once determination sets in, it is a wrap — it is happening, or I will die trying. I was determined to overcome the statistics stacked up against me on every level. My teachers' and elders' wisdom rang in my head to tell me that I can still achieve my goals even if the journey may look a little different; I can do all this through the Messiah that strengths me. As I regain my composure, after my brief insanity to abort the assignment I have in this realm, I looked down at my son. I took accountability for my part in the situation I had gotten myself into and forgave myself for the rest. I started reading the scriptures and exercising physically to combat the depression to allow me to keep focus on something other than my immediate problems. I got quiet to listen.

Building my mental strength, I noticed a pattern within myself that I did every time I wanted to be better — do better. I came up with some questions when I wanted change for my life. I would think, "what is pulling me to want this change?" I can remember going to the hospital all the time with migraines. I suffered horribly even with a high pain tolerance. It was so bad, the doctors had to put me on four or five intense mediations at once for me to even feel any relief. Talking to the nurse one night after five hours of sleep, she stated stress may have been the cause of my situation. I looked back to realize the only time I got to sleep peacefully was at the hospital or my childhood home. There were no twenty-hour days, no fights, no drama, no drugs, no strangers, no threats in those places. Not being in that environment allowed me to sleep. I needed change — peace was my motivation.

I got a plan to get myself and my child in a healthier living environment — the goal: my first apartment. I asked myself, "how do we get the peace we need?" A place of our own. Well, I am not scared of a job. So, putting the rubber to the road, job hunting I went. Occupational therapy helped me regain some of my confidence that I had lost. I was around elders that poured into me and people that really liked me as a person. Interacting with people at work helped me battle with my depression. My job gave me a sense of purpose everyday which allowed my mind to think beyond the beating that was waiting at home - I was learning and growing. My life was not glamorous by far however, I was able to start meeting my essential needs without depending on others to do it. I planned all the time and created weekly, monthly and yearly goals for my family. I am sucker for celebrating the small wins each and every time. I remember having to save up a whole year for a $60 pair of new shoes — white reebok classics. Yes, you read that right — a year. I was that broke but honey you could not tell me nothing when I purchased them. I put my children in front of my needs and wants, so now I was determined to splurge on myself. It seems like little to some, but a whole lot for others. I did not have much in my first apartment, just a mattress, but it was all mine. I mopped those floors every night with pride. My mind could finally get a chance to heal. I was able to deal and process what just happened the last couple of years of life adulthood. In the mix, I found myself as a single parent co-parenting with an inmate. What do I do now? I am a part of the 10% of African American women supporting their children's father while incarcerated. There is no rule book for this parenting thing, let alone a SINGLE parent handbook that I could find.

You cannot stay in the pity party you created for yourself. Give it attention to recognize and identify the problem then place attention to how you will go about solving it. Many get stuck in the place of figuring it out. Well I am here to tell you that you do not have to have all of the answers. One step is all you have to figure out at that moment. How can you make a healthy shift to remove yourself from the situation you do not like for yourself or your life? What does a healthy step even look like? If you find yourself not knowing what a health environment looks like, utilize your local library for self-help books in this area. Your healthy step forward in this instance would be to figure out what is healthy even look like to you. Self-help books can guide you to self-revelation to answer this question for yourself. Once a healthy idea is established think about your next healthy step, and/or steps, you are going to use to step outside a toxic environment. I went to school to get my degree so I can be able to take care of my new budding family. This shift in my thinking required me to sort things out and working to understand how I got here and ensure that I never have to go back to that kind of life again. Remember my children are going to have what I was not able to experience myself. I want better for them. I was determined for them to overcome the statistics.

I am a true believer of what you go through gives someone hope and strength and energy to endure their time in their season to show them to keep on keeping on. Those days in my father's dry cleaners taught me so many things that kept me alive while surviving. I was able to learn to relate to others from all walks of backgrounds. My childhood prepared me to be able to run a state meeting with the Vice President attending to speak with a murderer. I had what I needed already inside of me and it was ready to be cultivated. Being new to this adult thing, you run into characters. I had plenty of time to self-reflect, no cable or tv in the apartment, so my spiritual eye was strengthened over time. I was in the dark as to what the gift I possessed; however, I was aware of its existence. Having your life surrounded by those that do not carry light, you tend to have your light dimmed. I had the pattern to fix things and make things better. Growing professionally, every business I encountered grew financially with my suggestions, however, I noticed everyone around me was not genuinely happy for me. When you are involved with someone who does not know themselves, that tends to project into your sanity. I saw that consistently and often wondered why.

My journey with men as a serial monogamous has not been the easiest. I was a part of the generation that was stubborn and had to figure things out for myself. This person is different; love conquers all with rose colored glasses all the way. The unconditional love I was taught really is conditional at the end of the day. It must be. I will unconditionally love you until you violate my condition of loving me with respect and honor. In my observation about business and happiness, I notice this was the violation that had occurred. The delicate balance of the unconditional versus conditional love showed up when I got my first apartment. My children's father was sent to prison and I was alone; I was left to parent the children that were assigned to me to make great. I had a lot of anger towards the new path our family had to take. This was not a part of the plan. This was not supposed to be my life. I was supposed to have the dark and handsome husband that adored me, our children and the dream house – the American dream (or nightmare – however you look at it). However, there I was, sitting with nothing in my possession and two beings looking towards me for the answers. At this point, I naturally took the reins of his position in his immediate family - why would I not, I was his Empress!

I knew him like the back of my hand and 90% of the time knew how he would respond to any situation. He was me and I was he – universally one. We just had that understanding; speaking without talking – just the eyes. His burden of carrying his whole family, immediate and extended, fell on me. We were not married, but it became my responsibility to represent him to the fullest. I worked hard to support everyone – him, his family and my family too. When I thought about making money unconventionally, I was able to reach down inside to pull out a way to get us something to eat that night instead. I ate water sandwiches. I was willing to walk miles to work, just so my children can enjoy childhood pleasures. I remember not having heat for a couple of weeks. I had the children in the living room huddled together. Their father was incarcerated at this point, so we wrote each other daily plus calls. I had at least 300 letters I was keeping for later sentimental reasons. As painful as it was, I watched every letter burn for us to stay warm that night and the next. It was not easy at all.

One day he asked me something unfathomable that required me to take from our children. At that moment, I hit that big wall of reality – I cannot love a man more than my well-being. Self- sacrifice and becoming a martyr for someone's growth does yourself a disservice in the lack of growth within yourself. It leaves you in a box with the opinionated, every changing, walls of the person of your affection. If only I took just an ounce of energy, I put towards giving to the men in my life I will be in a much different place in my life. I realize that now. I had a moment of interreflection to gain clarity on what the initial version of my future I had for myself. I had to stop and take consideration of my present circumstances. I really evaluated how I was going to adjust the vision I had for myself to a modified way of living my life. What is the plan for my life now? I had to project a new vision. I consistently go through this process now every year. This process has never failed me thus far. Even though I lost numerous jobs, because I had no help at that time; I was able to take myself through school to obtain a degree, create several businesses that I am passionate about along with the soul purpose mission. I have no other choice but to surround myself with go getters.

The Most High has given His people power over the principalities and dark entities of this world. It is not abnormal to love passionately with all purity. The world wants you to think that way; to pervert what is real to make you feel less than what your true powers have ordained you to become. The chosen are given tools, guides and wisdom to battle this world. We are here to sharpen one other and push each other to be great. Our journey contains assignments given to each of us to stretch and grow. In these trials, you gain wisdom to be better. Write the vision, make it plain. Do the work. Activate your destiny.

Patrice "Foxy" Johnson, PMP/MBA/MHA

Patrice is a successful IT business executive who manages global resources and is a highly regarded IT leader with a big heart to serve her community. In addition, she is a travel entrepreneur, teaching others to build wealth through travel. Her career yields many great opportunities to travel and meet people from all over the world. Her background and focus on community outreach and collaboration has led to a number of motivational speaking engagements, volunteer opportunities and community leadership roles. She is a recognized community Board Member and successful business activist. She has a tremendous love to help and uplift others. Beyond her career progression she is also a female motorcyclist. Infamously known as "Foxy" within the Motorcycle Community, Foxy is the General Manager for the MC Professional Convention aka "The PROC", Chair for the NC ALL Female Ride Committee and NC Ambassador for Black Girls Ride the Movement. She enjoys and has great passion for educating and helping bikers. She is also an avid female motorcycle activist, serving in various roles with the motorcycle culture. Riding has become a past time, and she loves to ride the distance. She enjoys meeting and greeting fellow bikers on various ground pounding road trips. She has been riding for decades and is committed wholeheartedly. HONDA will forever be her first love; she is now a Honda/Harley hybrid biker babe. Patrice has years of mentoring youth and young adults to lifelong success.

Although she thoroughly enjoys her career and being an avid female biker; family comes first and she loves being a wife to a great husband of 27 years - Don aka Disel, mother to 2 awesome young men, and grandmother to two adorable grandsons.

Patrice's Dedication:

To the village who help mold my life in becoming the bold, confident woman:

The kinfolks who raised me — my awesome mother Sarah and father Paul, my deceased grandparents Charles and Rosa Bell, aunts Mary (deceased), Cora, Rosa, uncles Charles, Ernest (deceased), Nathaniel, Harrison, Walter large extended family.

My dare to be different circle of sisters and women who always empower and motivate me to greatness, my loyal friends who uplift in every way.

To the loves of my life

DJ and Patrick my two true blessings who make me the woman I am today. Kayden and Amari my wonderful grandsons who continue to define me being a mom. And finally, Donald my amazing and awesome husband who provides unconditional love and molds my strength in being a mom and a wife.

Introduction:

Always boldly declare that all things and promises of God are possible and life can be lived abundantly. You have the power beyond and actions you embark upon to declare victory into the Kingdom of God or be derailed by bondage and turmoil; which will you choose. Greatness is upon you and no matter how your life starts you can define your path and what your legacy will say for you. Know that nothing is impossible for you so go forth and lay a path and trail for others to follow.

Connect with Patrice

Phone: 919-423-3268

Website: www.getuse2travel.com
Email: getuse2travel@yahoo.com

CHAPTER 15

Be the Break of Barriers

To the great readers of the world, I am Patrice Johnson aka Foxy with a story to share and provide a testimony to the saying "You don't have to be a product of your environment". Born in 1971 to a mother who was a senior in college, one of nine children, third child, first to go to college and the oldest girl, life has not always been easy but to God be the Glory it is well worth it. You see, I was conceived on a college campus by a young student in her senior year of college. At the time she had no idea how her parents would accept her pregnancy and contemplated time and time again what their reaction would be if finding out. Being a college student in the seventies did not afford children the option to stay on campus during school breaks and off campus housing was not as popular nor affordable for most. My grandparents were sharecroppers living in the rural Mars Bluff Community of Florence, S.C. They did not have much money but made do with what they had; after all, having nine children was not an easy task to tackle. The life being lived was endured in the back of the woods off Hwy 301 in what many may refer to as a shack - a home with a tin roof with holes, no doorknobs nor locks, and floors which allowed you to see the ground. Everything the family ate came from outside, from vegetables and fruits to meats and nuts. Those were the gold 'ole days of eating.

My mom coming home for holiday break in 1970 was the initial acceptance of my being on earth. Immediately upon her departure off the bus, my grandmother knew she was expecting. To hear the comforting words from her parents not that of disappointment but that of support saying, "you will do two things - have this baby and graduate," was soothing to her soul. My mother, a senior in college, was determined to do both. My life was not one accepted by the biological father, however having a caring grandfather and a few years later gaining a stepfather filled all voids. You see, children do not ask to come into this world and once they are here their lives should be treated with care. My biological father was caught up with campus life, being a baseball star and enjoying his frat life and having a child did not fit in for him. To God be the Glory my mother along with her parents cared enough about my life to see me all the way through.

February 24, 1971 I was born, and life began on a journey of the unknown. May 1972 my mom became the first child in the family on both sides to graduate from college. Life was not easy, but every experience has all been worth it. My mom moved to the North East as the starting pay for educators was much more in the North East than that of the South. During her time moving my grandparents took on the task of raising me to allow my mom to get a start on life. I was raised with my mom's younger siblings while my mom started her career. My grandfather would always say:

"It's not how you start it's how you finish."

Life yielded many ups and downs but nothing that was too big to overcome. The first twelve years of life started in the back woods of Florence, SC on a farm with my now deceased grandparents. From Florence, SC I moved to the Northeast Brick City hood of East Orange, N.J. Life yielded the struggles of the South and North but would not deny my life to be prosperous for my Father God has always been in the midst. Always intrigued by education I pursued a lifelong student journey to fulfill the desire to excel in my calling. So, one may ask why I moved to the Northeast?

After a flawless grade school experience, I entered middle school to then have my first experience with bullying. While many children fall prey to the bully, I was raised to never allow anyone to lay hands on me without defending myself. I had a major encounter coming off the school bus full of students. The bully of the community attacked me with a knife from behind; my mind when in several directions. As I was nipped on the belly with the first stabbing attempt, by the time the knife was being brought down I had taken my penny loafer shoe off and connected the heel with the knife of the bully and before I knew it, I had knocked the bully completely unconscious in a pool of blood. At a moment's notice my life flashed before me. After being pulled from the body of the bully by my cousin, who too was on the school bus, I was taken home to my grandmother. My grandmother was shaking as to be expected but confident that the occurrence had to be due to me being attacked. Given my grandmother was aging, my mother, who lived in East Orange, NJ, thought it would be best for me to move North and come back to spend my summers in the South. Moving to the Northeast was not what I wanted and of course felt I was being penalized for defending myself. Adjustment to a new life in the Northeast came quick and fast. The food was different, the attitudes of the people was different, no longer the southern charm and the home was different. Having to attend a new school and make new friends was the new challenge. Many students greeted me with my "country accent" as they would say, with open arms. I quickly got acquainted with my new surroundings but still had the SOUTH on my mind. For anyone struggling with adjustment in life, understand you have the perseverance built within you to succeed. I went from the farm, to the hood to sitting in Corporate Boardrooms. Although life through many curveballs along the way, I would not change a thing as it was a part of God's plan for my life. My high school experience allowed me to meet my husband and my college experience allowed me to meet professors who blessed me with continued articulation and public speaking skillsets.

Life today is beautiful. I am the second-generation undergraduate school graduate. I obtained a second undergraduate degree from Saint Augustine College (now University) as a salute to my mom who conceived me on that campus. Ironically enough the experience of getting this degree afforded me the opportunity to meet many of my mom's former classmates who were professors. I am a first-generation graduate school graduate (Summa Cum Laude) with double Master's Degrees. I am the first African American Woman to hold an executive Global IT Director position for an SAP Partner.

To go from being raised by sharecroppers to earning well into six figures has been a true confirmation you do not have to be a product of your environment and can define a path of success. Today I am a business owner, entrepreneur and IT executive which affords me the ability to reach back and grab others who are battling the struggles from their current environment. It gives me great pleasure to build a dynasty to teach others how to become financially independent and retire early. To my almighty God be the GLORY.

Shereka Lindsey

 Shereka Lindsey is a preacher, wife (married to James Lindsey), mother of two (Ja'Nae and Jayvin), correctional officer and an author. Whatsoever her hands can find to do she will do it.

Shereka was born on January 21, 1979 to Laura Spencer and Larry Drakeford. God has blessed her with two sisters Tiphanie and Keyana Drakeford who are great supporters. She graduated from Pinecrest High in 1997 and is currently enrolled to becoming a Voice Actor. The sky is the limit.

God called her to step out in ministry in the year 2002; she stood up before her church along with other believers to declare the Word of God. Since that time, she has been serving at the House of Prayer in Taylortown, N.C. This Woman of God is headed to the next level and currently creating a Podcast. The future is filled with many possibilities.

Shereka's Dedication

This chapter is dedicated to God and Duke University Hospital. When my husband and I began this journey of taking care of our son, Jayvin, we were aware it would be a challenge since we already have a 2-year-old daughter but did not know all we would have to go through. In order to master this trial, we were facing, we teamed together to do what needed to be done. A greater force of help was needed to help him medically as we turned to God and Duke University Hospital. God is giving us the strength we need. Duke University we love you and appreciate you helping us every step of the way. The doctors and nurses were willing to answer any questions we had as well provide resources to better help his development. You will never understand how grateful we are. May God continue to bless you!

Connect with Shereka:

Phone: 910 690 3481

Email: sherekadrakeford@yahoo.com

CHAPTER 16
IT WAS NOT A MISTAKE, BUT INTENTIONAL!

30% of Down syndrome babies who are not terminated end up a miscarriage or stillbirth. Six thousand babies are born with Down Syndrome every year. Our names came up and we got handpicked by God to care for such an angel. I was asked if I wanted to get rid of my unborn child by a professional doctor. It was not a mistake, but intentional, that in the month of April 2018 I was in my living room having family time with my Mom, one of my sisters, and my 1-year- old daughter at the time. (I have another sister who name is Tiphanie who is also a great supporter.) As we were sitting and laughing as usual, I felt the need to go take a pregnancy test. I did not have any symptoms whatsoever, but this was my normal. When I was pregnant with my daughter, I did not have any symptoms for about two months. I was shocked to find out that I was pregnant with her. My husband, James, and I had been trying for four years. After taking the test the results came up positive. My daughter Ja'Nae is now 2 years old and healthy. Now, after taking the second pregnancy test and finding out I was pregnant I was shocked again. This time we were not even trying to have another baby so soon. This time I was only three weeks pregnant. I had been to the beach, out there in the heat, with no clue that the Lord wanted to add to our family. Of course, we were excited to find out another addition to the family was on the way! My daughter, however, was not happy. She did not want to share her spotlight. Every time we mentioned her having a sister or brother she would yell "No!" We went to the doctor after some time had passed to find out we are having a boy. Wow, I felt honored to be able to have a girl and a boy!!! God was shining on our family as the smiles and the jumping for joy continued. Soon after, we received the news that our baby boy was going to be born with Down Syndrome.

Like most parents who have a Down syndrome child your first thought is "What did I do wrong?"; you also wonder "Is God mad at me?" I know it sounds crazy to think that way. When you begin to think about what it takes to raise a child with special needs your mind begins to spin. Lord am I equipped to handle this? What will he have to go through physically? Do we have the finances to cover the medical bills? James and I were so overwhelmed that we said to ourselves that the doctor must have made a mistake. We said, "Surely, he misread the ultrasound!" This brought us to our knees and into a place of prayer; we got spiritual quick to get insight on what God was up to. We started talking faith and said, "when our son is born, they will see they were wrong." We carried this belief all through the pregnancy believing God for a miracle. A few months before giving birth to our son God began to speak. He let us know the doctor was right and He had a plan. He intended for my son to be born with Downs (short term for Down syndrome).

After going on a few doctor appointments, a doctor asked me if I wanted to abort my baby. The question alone was hard to process. In my mind I said, "How could you ask me to kill my own child? How could you ask me to get rid of what God created?" I could not have that blood on my hands. Despite hearing that Jayvin had Down Syndrome, we still wanted to love this child like any other child; whatever we had to go through we were up for the challenge. The appointments went from checking his development to preparing for heart surgery. It appeared so much was coming our way, but there were decisions to be made and he was not even here yet.

I have never prayed so much in my life. Knowing the task that was at hand had me on bended knees. God knows how to get you to pray. Walking with Christ is a daily walk that takes daily communication. Sure, our lives get busy, but we should never be too busy to pray and communicate with God. As time passed, I continued to pay close attention to what this trial was trying to teach my husband and I. The Lord had a purpose for what was taking place and it was up to us to pay attention and get this lesson. It was not enough to know there would be multiple doctor appointments, but adding to the weight, we had to travel an hour and a half for these appointments to Duke University Hospital in Durham, NC. I am talking about time, gas, and co-payments each time.

Jayvin was born January 4, 2019. He went straight from my womb to the ambulance to be taken to the children's hospital. I did not get to hold him and cuddle like most moms. He needed medical attention right away; the prayers of the righteous availeth much and we had prayer warriors praying everywhere. People were praying in different states for the well-being of our baby. There were people praying and I did not even know their names. It was amazing to see God bring people together to pray for this innocent soul. My husband and I knew before he was born there would be some complications, but I never imagined not being able to bring him home right away. It had not crossed my mind that I would not be able to bond with my own child. This day the Lord let me know Jayvin belonged to Him and that he is chosen to carry out a special mission. My eyes were opened to see the glory of God being manifested. Even though I was hurt I knew God was in control. God has a way of testing your faith even when you feel like you are so close to Him and you believe in Him. Things will take place in your life to show you just how much you truly believe. I thought I was praying before, but this prayer took me to the threshing floor.

We get to the hospital the next day to see my baby in ICU. Yes, I said the next day. I had a C-section and still had to be treated as a patient. It did not make sense for me to be in one hospital while he was in another. He had trouble with his breathing due to being born with an AV heart condition. He was born with jaundice, bleeding on the brain and was not able to eat on his own; there was no interest whatsoever to eat so a feeding tube had to be placed in his stomach. So much was going on at one time it was mind blowing. The same God I had trusted all these years was the same God allowing this to happen. Where was He now while we were being strong for Jayvin? Was He not hearing our prayers? Did our praying not matter? Of course, it did, and we realized it when we looked around in the hospital rooms to see we were not the only ones going through this. We were not alone. Sometimes you feel like you are going through that trial or test all by yourself, but someone is going through it in the same way if not worse. We learned there were several parents facing the same test and some had been going through this for months if not a year. Here we were complaining and feeling like God had abandoned us and these poor people are still waiting on an answered prayer. God was showing us favor and letting us see we needed to take the focus from us and start praying for others as well. Do you see where I am going with this? We go before God as believers and pray a prayer only for ourselves when there is more to pray about. You trust God and you believe in Him, but what about those that do not pray and believe? Who will cry for them? Who will turn the plate down and fast and pray for their situation? Are you so selfish to only pray for yourselves and not pray and be there for others?

A month had passed, and we spent the whole month of January at the hospital waiting and praying for a miracle. His healing was taking place and quick. We went home for about two and a half months then it was happening all over again. The respiratory issues began, and we had to take Jay back to the hospital for further treatment. I was just beginning to bond with him and learning his ways when two viruses had made their way into his lungs making it hard to

200

breathe so back to the ICU my little man went. He was placed in ICU to get high flow oxygen and a few medications and was hospitalized for three weeks. I felt like I had made God mad! Where did I go wrong? I begin to search my life over to see what I did to cause this. I took this visit personal and once again we called on the prayer warriors to help us pray. Once again God showed me this was His business and I needed to attend to His business and not create my own. (Oh yes, when you give your life to Christ you give it completely to Him.) My prayer before any of this took place was "Lord I want to be a Christian from the heart, and I want to get a closer relationship with Him." There are prayers we pray and it seems like God is not listening then there are those prayers that according to your faith God answers immediately; I mean you must laugh to keep from crying. Oh yes, He has a comical side. My husband and I traveled up and down the road to Durham every day to be with my son. The hospital was an hour and a half away. By this time God really began to show up even financially through churches, my family, my co-workers and people I did not know. My best friend Kim, my co-worker Lieutenant Gillard and Kenny Green began a fund raiser on Jayvin's behalf to help us with the bills, gas, and medications; a Go Fund Me account, ticket raffle and a bike ride was done on his behalf. Yes, we have insurance, but that does not pay for everything our precious angel requires. The Lord was letting us know through His people, "you may be going through this, but I have your back."

Towards the end of April, we went home again for about a week. My son was having some pain and was very uncomfortable. I could not figure out exactly where the pain was so yes, you guessed it, back to the hospital we went. This time his feeding tube had become infected as well as some respiratory issues. He was born with fluid on his lungs, so this was an ongoing problem. As we ran into the month of May 2019 the doctors decided to go ahead and do the heart surgery, May 22nd to be exact. They were ready to cut my baby, but again God said, "This is My son!" I cannot argue with God nor do I want to. In places like this, the doubts tend to show up: Am I making the right choice by letting them do the surgery? The flesh will kick in, but do not allow it to take the place of God. The spirit is willing, but the flesh is weak.

May 22nd, 2019 the doctors proceeded to do surgery. I was not worried because these were some of the best Doctors at Duke University Children's Hospital. After a few hours had passed, one of the doctors wanted to take us into a room to counsel us on what was going on and how the surgery went. The surgery was a success however his heart was not strong enough to come off the bypass machine; no worries God's got it all in control. His chest had to remain open until his heart became stronger. When I walked into the room to see my baby laying there with his chest open and unconscious motherhood stood up in me. My faith was still alert, and I trusted God to bring him out completely. I wanted to hold him in my arms to let him know mommy was here and everything was going to be alright. My baby had no clue he was even in the world. Full of morphine, sedated and resting we just sat and prayed as God continued to heal his heart. I asked the Lord to charge his angels at bedside to watch over him and of course He did just that.

Three days had passed. It was time for my baby to start waking up. Watching this miracle take place before my eyes was amazing. He could not open his eyes, but he couldn't wiggle. After a few more days I was able to see those bright eyes. I was not able to hold him during this process and felt like we were being robbed of our bonding time. We were able to rub his head and place our finger in his hand. You must look at the positives you are given and refuse to allow the devil to take your blessing. The threshing floor was a place we could really go to God and sincerely express what was on our hearts. When you are on that threshing floor it gets real as the tears, spit, and mucus all come out. This is the place where it is proven: You mean business with the Lord.

A few more weeks had gone by as he was in recovery. We watched God heal Jayvin as he also healed our hearts. Even though our baby was the one who had surgery it was our hearts that was being changed. Our lives are changed forever even now as we continue to press forward. After recovering from this test, we were able to come home and began the bonding process all over again. We felt complete because Jay was home at last, but it was not over yet. He had to have a routine check to ensure everything was going as expected, but on our way to the appointment his oxygen tank malfunctioned. At the time I had no idea that it happened. I knew his breathing had changed and he was in duress. It was mind blowing to witness it happening all over again. I was nervous and I knew we would not return home as planned. The doctor checked him out and said, "Mrs. Lindsey I am so sorry to have to tell you this, but I have to send him back into the hospital. It appears he has more fluid on his lungs," My head dropped; however, I was not surprised. I could not understand why this was happening again. It was unreal to have to tell the family we were headed back to Duke for the fifth time. Maybe we had not trusted God enough or our faith did not take us as far as we hoped. What was going on? Was it a lesson we failed to learn from? So many questions were in my head. I had to go back to what God said in the beginning. This is not a mistake, but intentional! Everything that was taking place was all a part of the plan. At this point we learned to relax and let God drive. You cannot predict the outcome, but you can determine your response to what is happening. A lot of us tell God what we want without asking Him what the plan is. The threshing floor will teach us not to just go in prayer asking for what we want, but to listen to what God is saying; hear His voice and harden not your hearts.

The battle is not over, but victory has been won. Jayvin is now showing interest in wanting to eat, roll over and even grab for objects. He is currently on oxygen all day, but we are believing God for a miracle. One day he will not need the oxygen to function. Some angels are seen and some we cannot see. I know God placed several angels at Duke University Hospital and there were several assigned to Jayvin. To some they looked like normal people, but when you open the eyes of your heart you can see God moving. I watched as they cared for him as though he were their own; some fell in love with him and wanted to take him home. The love that was shown toward all of us was heartwarming. I had even considered changing my career to become a nurse because I was so inspired. The road ahead of us will be challenging, but we have so much love and support from family, friends, and outside resources.

You can plan all through life what you would like to happen not knowing what the outcome will be. Things are going to happen. How are you prepared to handle it? Another thing the Lord has taught me is it is important how you respond to what you go through. If you are negative the whole time your outcome will be negative. You have to say to yourself, "I am going to get out of this." Seeing Jayvin go through all this could have caused me to lose faith, however I knew we needed help. Trials come to strengthen us not tear us down; we must keep fighting regardless of what we are facing. Some have had it harder than others, but no matter what, you must fight with your faith, heart, mind, and spirit. God gives us what we need to keep fighting. What if we would have stopped fighting for Jayvin? What if we stop believing in God? This trial was not about us. It was about fighting for Jayvin. Some women lose hope before the baby is born by killing the baby in the womb. Even if you cannot take care of the blessing God has given you, it does not give you the right to destroy it; give the child to someone who can. Every child whether "normal" or not, deserves a fighting chance because they have purpose for being here. Knowing Jayvin was going to need medical attention and we had to get others involved to help us raise him was overwhelming, but we had to look ahead. Sure, we were in denial in the beginning and we had hoped the doctor was making a mistake. We wanted Jayvin to be as normal as his sister. We wanted him to go to school and not have to worry about why he is different from others. No matter what we wanted, that was not what God's plan is. Now, we are so excited to see who this child will turn out to be. He is getting stronger every day. We are his support team along with everyone else who fights for him daily. Fighting is not getting revenge or showing someone how strong or smart you think you are. Fighting is recognizing the situation and facing it head on with prayers to God and supplying the faith for Him to work with. Do you want a miracle? Give Him something to work with. When God looks at you, He needs to see Himself, not someone who gives in to defeat. When you communicate with the Lord daily, He supplies you with what you need. We can get through this by talking with Him daily, staying in His word and committing to fasting and prayer. Do not try to be like anyone else, but instead, be who He wants you to be. People go through things differently; however, we have the same source who supplies our needs. He promised to always be with us and to never forsake us. He is not like man who will disappoint or forsake you. Stay on bending knees and be faithful to Him.

Some things we will not be able to avoid, however we can be equipped through the word of God and through prayer. I am really stressing this to let you all know that there is no way my husband and I could have gotten through this and continue to get through this without the power prayer and keeping this posture of prayer before Him. I do not want to sound like a broken record, but someone really needs to hear this because there is someone who is trying to do this on their own and that is impossible. The Bible is not a fictional book; the things that happen in there are very real; even to this day we are still experiencing some of the things that they went through. It may not be popular to live a clean and holy life however there is a reward to all of those who dare to believe and follow this straight and narrow way. The choice is yours. Choose now or lose out.

I would not trade my children for anything in this world. They are so dear to me and my husband James. If I had a choice to give my child Jayvin away to avoid the challenges that we face I would still choose to keep my child and keep fighting. I feel as though as I am writing someone is ready to give up in the fight, but God is stressing to you this day to not give up. There are many of you who will be reading this, and you understand completely what I am going through because your child or children have a disability. This message is to encourage you and to let you know that God is on your side and that your child is not a mistake, but it was intentional for that child to be born. Now, that the blessing is here it is your responsibility to take care of the blessing and watch the miracle manifest itself. To God be all the Glory for the great things He has done and will continue to do.

Melanie Palmer

Melanie Palmer is a graduate of James Benson Dudley High School and North Carolina Agricultural & Technical State University, earning a Bachelor of Arts degree in Psychology in 2001. She returned in 2004 to be a part of the Project Pisces Cohort specializing in licensure in Special Education.

Mrs. Palmer was a Special Education teacher for ten years and recently was appointed to serve in an administration role for the past five years. She has been contracted to host various workshops such as Praxis Review, Data Manipulation, EC Paperwork, & Implementing Behavior Intervention Plans Most recently, Mrs. Palmer has been asked to serve on the board of Project Creed (Culturally Responsive Exceptional Educators for Diversity). In addition, she is a member of several civic and professional organizations.

Mrs. Palmer has been married to her high school sweetheart, Ahmad for the past 18 years. Together, they have one daughter, Makiya.

Melanie's Dedication

To my Daddy: For showing me what a great educator
should look like;

To my Husband: For assisting me in being a great educator;

To my Daughter: For allowing me to be a great educator!

Connect with Melanie

Phone: 336-908-5521

Email: akababyrl04@gmail.com

CHAPTER 17

God's Triumph

In the summer of 2001, I had graduated from college, married my high school sweetheart, and moved to California to begin my new life. Within a year, I gave birth to my only child. On the outside looking in, one would think that I was on top of the world! Well, that was far from the truth and my perfect world, all changed within a time span of three years.

On September 11, 2001, the United States of America experienced one of the worst tragedies that anyone could ever imagine when terrorists decided to hijack four of our planes crashing them into the Twin Towers of the World Trade Center, a surrounding area and the other close to the Pentagon. My husband, who was a Lance Corporal in the United States Marine Corp, was immediately sent to an undisclosed location for a few months and would end up being a part of Operation Iraqi Freedom. One day, I received a phone call stating that there had been fatalities within his squadron, and I needed to stay at home to wait for the Chaplain to arrive. There, I was a new mother, wife, and I am literally across the country without any family members or close friends nearby, waiting to hear if my husband was one of the marines that paid the ultimate sacrifice for our freedom. By the grace of God, the chaplain never came to my house and I was able to breathe a sigh of relief! As fate would have it, my husband did lose a few close friends so, a decision was made that my husband would finish his term with the Marine Corp, and we would move back to our hometown to raise our daughter.

After much discussion, it was decided that I would return home a year prior to my husband, to work on finding a job and place for us to live. When I returned home, I stayed with my parents until our house was built. During this time, I read the paper daily, searched the internet, and attended job fairs. I quickly learned that having a Bachelor of Arts degree in Psychology, was not adequate, when applying for various positions. After several days of searching, I came across an ad for a teacher's assistant position within the public-school system in the area I lived. I was called in for an interview and hired on the spot; the principal loved my candor and thought I would be a great fit with the teacher of record! In August of 2004, I started my career in the education field. This is something that I had always told myself that I would never do, due to the lack of compensation. My goal was to work and attend school at night to get my graduate degree in Psychology. My dream was to have my own practice, as a licensed Psychologist. Everything was going according to plan; I was back at home with my family and friends, saving money by living with my parents, and was able to secure a job within three months of being back.

So, the 2004-2005 school year has started, and I am an assistant in a self-contained classroom for students with disabilities. I love the students, the lead teacher, and the overall makeup of the school. I am starting to have a change of heart and realize that I love working with children. Months have passed and, becoming more driven to learn more about the education field, I begin asking questions. I want to do more than I am allowed inside of the classroom however, the atmosphere has changed! The dynamic of the relationship between the lead teacher and I have changed! Rumors arise that I am asking too many questions, I do not like be around the children, I am lazy, and not a good fit for (HER) classroom! I made the decision to sit down and have a conversation before things took a turn for the worse. The following questions were asked: "Is there a problem with my performance? Are there things that you would like for me to do different? Would you like to have another assistant assigned to this class?" The answer to every question was, NO! A few weeks go by and a district employee, whom I had the pleasure of meeting previously, came into the classroom and pulled me to the side. She shares with me that my performance inside of the classroom has impressed her and that she would like for me to consider going back to school for Special Education. She also states that she is currently on the board for a grant that would pay all of my expenses should I decide to change my major. When I return to work the following day, the lead teacher inside of my classroom, tells me that the same district employee informed her that I lacked in my performance and needed to be on an action plan to correct it. Perplexed, I asked, "How could that be? Why would she recommend me to be a part of a new cohort and think that my performance is not up to par?" The teacher is stunned; her face is red, and her negative intentions are being realized and to add insult to injury, emails the district employee questioning my integrity. The devil did not win this battle and what was meant to stop and keep me from walking into the calling that God had put in place for me, did not prosper. In August 2005, I applied and was accepted into Graduate school with a major in Special Education.

The 2005-2006 school year has begun, and the lead teacher decides not to return for another year. Based on my rapport with the staff, students, and parents, I am asked to step up until a replacement was found. This was a blessing for me, as now I can practice my craft and show colleagues that I can lead the classroom in a positive direction. Everything is going great and the end of the year is approaching; when DISASTER STRIKES! It was brought to my attention that one of the students in my classroom is hurt. I did what I was taught and followed procedures. Everything turned out great and the student was back the next day, however, a complaint is filed because some felt compassion was only shown from me and not others within the school; I tried my hardest to fix this situation; yet, the damage was done. As a result, an administrator turns her back on me and did everything in her power to ruin my reputation. The end of the school year is almost over, and I am now interviewing for teaching positions; everything is going great! I am dressed professionally, my portfolio speaks for itself, and I am answering questions with confidence. Before I left every interview, I am offered the position, however, as I return home, the offers are rescinded. This went on for another month and it never occurred to me that I was being blackballed. I began to question God about why He would bring me here just to turn His back on me? I maintained an "A" average all through school, had one of the highest Praxis scores, and my students' test scores were improving so needless to say I could not understand why this was happening. I went home every night feeling defeated. What am I supposed to do now? It never occurred to me that God was working in my favor and that those schools were not destined for me. It was an elementary school in the neighborhood that I grew up in that I received God's triumph. It was be there, that I would reunite with that same district employee who assisted me in going back to school. It was there that I met a principal who shared everything that was said yet chose to follow her heart and look at the facts. It was there that I would meet a group of women who would guide me into the educator that I am today.

It is now 2019 and I am still in the education field. I have taught students with disabilities from grades Kindergarten through 5. I served as chairman of my department and was elected teacher of the year. Currently, I am an administrator, teach on the college level, tutor, and serve on the same board as my mentor to write grants for students who would like to become Special Education Teachers. This is something that I never imagined would be my path but look at how God worked everything out in my favor!

My advice to others who have experience setbacks such as this, is to never give up. God will never put more on you than you can bear nor will he ever leave you! Regardless of what you are going through, it is never outside of his reach. For those who considered being an educator and think that it is too far out of reach or have other concerns, it is a great field of study and can be very rewarding. It is time to prepare the next generation of doctors, lawyers, engineers, and EDUCATORS! Therefore, we must have a "Team I" mentality and understand that "NO WEAPON FORMED AGAINST YOU SHALL PROSPER!"

Gresha Williams

MBA, MHA

Gresha Williams is a native of Greensboro, North Carolina. She has progressed through a series of corporate positions despite the challenges that she has faced throughout her life. Gresha is currently the Director of Supply Chain Operations for a leading healthcare company in the Southeast. She manages daily supply chain operations for multiple procedure areas in fourteen medical centers.

Gresha received her Bachelor of Arts degree in Business Administration from the University of North Carolina at Greensboro. She received a Master of Business Administration (MBA) and a Master of Health Administration (MHA) from Pfeiffer   University.

Gresha serves as a Diversity and Inclusion facilitator for her current employer. In this role she facilitates difficult conversations with team members to create and sustain change that fosters a more creative, inclusive, respectful, and creative workplace. She holds two certifications: Certified Pharmacy Technician (CPhT) and Certified Materials Resource Professional (CMRP).

Pregnant at the age of sixteen, giving birth at the age of seventeen and having four children by the age of twenty-three, Gresha has beat society's stereotype of a teenage mother. Her passion for writing is to inspire other teenage mothers who feel their dreams are deferred due to their circumstances.

This book is dedicated to my four children TaTiana, Jaran II, Jada, and Jamel-you all are the best thing that has ever happen to me. My drive to succeed in life and accomplish my goals is because of you. All I ever wanted to do is to provide a great life for each of you. I hope momma has made you proud! I love you!

To my best friend Mary Katherine Jones also known as "My Granny" may you rest in peace. Thank you for being there for me when no one else was. You showed me the true definition of unconditional love. I promise to keep pushing and keep God first in everything I do. I miss you!

To my family and close friends thank you for always supporting me; I love each one of you.

Connect with Gresha

P.U.R.E. Events & Decor

Phone: 980-253-9195

Website: www.pureeventsanddecor.com

Facebook: https://m.facebook.com/pureeventsanddecor

IG: https://www.instagram.com/pureeventsanddecor/

CHAPTER 18

The Ultimate Sacrifice

Most of us live our lives based on other people's definition of success for us. It is important to define success for yourself, set goals and strive to reach those goals. It may not be an easy task due to obstacles that arise as God works to fulfill your dreams. There are many outside interferences that will distract you but stay focused on your goal and keep pushing. On this journey to success you will have to make many sacrifices along the way; just know that as you continue to step into your purpose a lot of things you used to do and people you used to hang around with will have to fall to the wayside. I am living proof that if you continue the path to success you define for yourself you will ultimately come out on top.

I remember the day that my kids' father and I decided to go our separate ways; I was devasted. There I was becoming a single mother of four children ages two, three, four, and seven. So many questions were going through my mind and I did not have an answer for any of them. I felt hopeless! The man that I spent nearly ten years of my life with was gone. Regardless of all the things that we had been through I still loved him from the bottom of my heart; he was my kids' father so why wouldn't I? The day that he left the house I remember him turning around and fixing his mouth to say, "You will never be anything. No one is going to want a single mother with four kids". My mouth dropped with disbelief. How could someone that loves you say those hurtful words? At that moment my heart had been crushed into a million pieces. I cried like a baby and fell into a deep depression. There were days that I could not pull myself out of bed. I would get up, fix food for the kids and crawl right back in the bed. I cut off family and friends because I did not want to hear those words, "I told you so". At work I would be happy and smiling but when I got home, I would be miserable. I was deeply hurting inside, and no one knew what I was going through but me. I knew that I could not stay in a depressed state too long because I was now the head of my household.

At the time I had a decent job in a community pharmacy working as a noncertified pharmacy technician. My checks paid the bills, but it did not provide the extra money I needed to provide for my kids. I needed a way to make fast and easy money, so I started looking into ways to make extra cash. I met a guy that was very popular in my hometown and was known for what the streets called "gettin money". I made deal with him that I would drive him around town to make his drug sales if he paid me one hundred dollars each time I drove. Easy money! I hooked up with a close friend of the family that sold what the streets call "weight". I would refer people I knew in the streets to him and make between a five hundred to one-thousand-dollar profit off each sale for sending them his way. Easy money! He would also drop bags of money off to me and pay me fifty dollars to count the bills in stacks of one thousand. Easy money! I would rent cars for a fee and once the person wanted to renew their rental again, I would charge an additional fee. Easy money! As I became more involved in illegal activity, I knew I had to find a legal way to make money. People around me were being picked up by the police and I knew for the sake of my kids I had to find a way out.

I remember coming home one day; I dropped to my knees to ask God for help. I knew that God had a better plan for my kids and I, but I had no clue what that plan would be. Not long after that I reconnected with one of my old friends who was locked up in federal prison at the time. At that moment I did not know that my prayer had been answered but looking back now the connection was destined. I would go visit him every week and we would talk for hours about life, goals, family, and entrepreneurship. The conversations we had helped me make the changes necessary for me to grow mentally,

218

physically, emotionally, and most important, spiritually. I began reading leadership books and educating myself on professional topics. Goal setting became my number one priority along with planning my weeks out accordingly. I quit procrastinating and took the time to become proactive. I began praying more and my faith in the word of God became stronger. My friends and family did not understand why I would want to support and visit someone in prison on a regular basis. I was intrigued; I never had anyone in my life that took the time to teach me about life lessons and what it took to be successful. I remember asking him the question, "What do you want from me? All men want something right?!" He answered, "What I want from you is to always better yourself. I want you to continue to be spiritually grounded. I want you to never be scared to take risks if you have done your homework on whatever it may be. I want you to be your best at all times." Those words gave me the encouragement and push I needed to go full throttle to the next level in my life. At that moment I felt that anything was possible. All I needed to do was set my mind on my goals and remove any distractions. It was only the beginning!

While my friends were partying and taking extravagant trips, I was trying to figure out what my next professional move was going to be. I begin thinking about how I could move up or even make more money at the community pharmacy I worked for. I learned that there was a National Certified Pharmacy Technician (CPhT) exam that I could take and if I passed, I would receive a raise. I was determined to pass this exam; I would go to work, pick the kids up from daycare, cook dinner, give them a bath, put them to bed and then study. On the weekend I would drop the kids off at my grandmother's house so I could get a couple of hours of studying done. This was my routine for months leading up to the day I had to take the exam. I am happy to say that CPhT became the first acronym following my name, but it would not be the last; accomplishing a goal,

I set for myself made me feel proud. I had gained the confidence I needed to continue to push forward to better my family. The sleepless nights and the sacrifices I had made paid off for the greater good. Although I received a raise I was still not satisfied where I was in my career. I begin to investigate the store manager training program and reached out to the district manager at the time to see what I needed to do to get on board. To my surprise, he was very impressed with me and when an assistant manager position opened, I was able to slide right into it. I had accomplished another goal that I set for myself; this open door became the catalyst I needed to begin working on the next goal on my list, a college degree.

I attended the University of North Carolina at Greensboro (UNCG) right out of high school, so I had a couple of classes already completed. I changed my major from nursing to business administration due to my interest shifting. I was working, going to school, taking care of my kids, and had work study. I had many sleepless nights and missed a lot of social functions, but my eye was always on the prize. I would use my refund check from school and my side hustle money to pay my bills up for the entire semester. I used my work check for my kids' clothes, shoes, and all other expenses. I may not have always looked up to par, but you better believe my kids did. Every time I would become discouraged, I would pull out my goal list and read over it repeatedly. This would help me refocus and stay on the right track. My grandmother was a big help with the kids and anytime I needed her she was there. It took me a little over two years to finish my degree. Another goal accomplished! At this point in my life I finally realized that I was no longer a "sayer" - I was now a doer.

After graduating from college, I left the community pharmacy and started working for a healthcare company where there was a lot more opportunity for me to move up in the corporate world. I started off in the Pharmacy as a certified pharmacy technician then moved up to a medication safety technician within two years. At work one day I came across a flyer that stated, "Learn how to earn your master's degree. Interest meeting will be held...". I attended the interest meeting, passed the entrance exam, and enrolled. I would go to work during the day and take classes in the evening at my current employer or at Moses Cone Hospital. Again, there were a lot of sleepless nights and social functions I was unable to attend but my eye was always on the prize. I realized that with working in the pharmacy department, there were not many opportunities available unless I went back to school to become a pharmacist. That was not happening! I started researching other departments within my organization to see what their career paths were. I found one department that stood out to me called "Supply Chain", so I reached out to the customer service manager to introduce myself. He was able to tell me more about the department and the career path available. At that moment I knew that supply chain was the place for me to be. A couple of weeks passed, and I received a call back from the same manager stating he had an open position and he would like to bring me in for an interview. Look at God! Soon after I started my new position, I earned my first master's degree. Another goal accomplished! Now with a Master of Health Administration in hand I was unstoppable. I started going above and beyond my assigned duties so I could be noticed by upper leadership within the department. I took on extra projects and looked for any processes that I could change to make the workflow more efficient. I sat with my manager, shared my career goals and asked him to be my mentor. My Granny always told me, "A closed mouth don't get fed". I put in the work and it paid off within a year. A supply chain manager position opened in the Charlotte market and guess who was asked to interview? Me!

The kids and I moved to the Charlotte, North Carolina area in 2012. As I began a new position within the organization, I kept the same process with evaluating how to reach my next professional goal. Within a year after moving to the Charlotte area I was promoted to a market supply chain manager over surgical services. Another goal accomplished! I went back to school to pursue a Master of Business Administration (MBA) which allowed me to become more competitive. In 2014, I was promoted to the Director of Supply Chain Operations for surgical services over the entire corporation. Another goal accomplished! In 2017, I studied and passed an exam to become a Certified Materials & Resource Professional (CMRP) which allowed me to become more competitive in the Supply Chain field. I have been blessed to overcome so many obstacles and come out on top!

I remember attending a leadership presentation and the following phrase stuck with me:

"If it is tied to you it dies with you".

It opened my eyes to see that what I have in my possession to leave my children when I am gone is not enough. I want them to lack nothing when I leave this earth - no worries at all. I want them to live in abundance for generations to come; at that moment I realized it starts with me! There were many times I wanted to throw in the towel, but God kept saying, "I got you! Keep pushing!"; my faith in Him is what kept me going. In 2019, I was able to open my very own event decorating company named after my late grandmother; P.U.R.E. Events & Décor. With the grace of God and support from my family and friends I am going to keep pushing until there are no goals left on my list.

On this journey called success some friends will make it to the end, and some will not. I had to separate myself from those who did not have the same goals as myself as they became distractions. They did not understand the demands my job required for me to move to the next level in the organization. As I become more successful my time became limited and attending social functions became slim to none. Some saw it as me "acting funny" or thinking I was better than them; for me, it was easier for me to just end some friendships instead of explaining myself repeatedly. It became draining and I needed to focus on what was beneficial for me and my kids. It hurts when your long-term friends do not support your career decisions and understand what you do for a living. For those individuals that I felt had my back one hundred percent and understood my goals, we made time to make it work.

As you continue on this journey called success it is essential to have healthy and happy relationships. You will continue to grow professionally and on a personal level which will transform friendships along the way. I always remember this quote from Tyler Perry's play Madea Goes to Jail:

"Some people are meant to come into your life for a lifetime, some for only a season and you got to know which is which. And you're always messing up when you mix those seasonal people up with lifetime expectations".

We all must travel through this thing called life. Always remember that the sky is the limit. At times your journey may be easy and at times it may be challenging. In order to know what path you need to take, you must define success for yourself and set goals to reach your dreams. On this journey you will have to make hard decisions that are best for you. There are going to be people that will not understand your decisions but always keep your eye on the prize. Do not be afraid to step outside the box to get what you want! Do you research. Have those uncomfortable conversations with professional people you may not know — those relationships will take you a long way. There are sacrifices that you will have to make but remember it will be well worth it in the end. Keep God first in everything you do. He will keep you well-grounded and in good spirits throughout your journey. Create a positive support system that will be there for you when you need help, advice and encouragement too. Keep your head high, keep striving, and keep winning because I am rooting for you. God bless!

Carol Danielle Craven

 Carol Danielle Craven is the third and youngest daughter of Colen and Bertha Craven. Craven is a North Carolina native who lived in New Carrolton, Maryland for 3 years where she became a published author, and small business owner of Southern Comfort by Carol, a Southern style cuisine catering service. She is the mother of four and a college graduate of the illustrious Shaw University with a B.A in Religion and Philosophy. She cherishes her family, children and entrepreneurial activities. She treasures her relationship with God and her theological community involvements.

Carol's Dedication
To my parents, children and grandchildren: Your ideas, wisdom and energy allowed me to persevere.

Connect with Carol
www.southerncomfortbycarol.org

336-965-9470

CHAPTER 19
All Consuming Grace

"Threshing is the process of loosening the edible part of grain (or other crop) from the husks & the straw to which it is attached. It is a step-in grain preparation and before winnowing, which separates the grain from the shaft."

February 11th, 2017 would be the start health of a health issue that would not be determined until August of that year. On the morning of that year I woke up feeling hot, nauseous and extremely tired, yet I pushed my way to work. Working in healthcare takes a special kind and push to keep going so I showered, dressed, had breakfast and hit the road. At the time I was living in New Carrolton, MD and was employed by hospice in Silver Spring, MD.

As the morning progressed, I began to feel worse. I keep going because my patients needed me and I needed them. Since I was five hours from home, my coworkers and patients became my family. In my mind going to work took precedence and I refused to leave my families in a state of confusion & without services. Little did I know at the time that making the choice to work would prove fatal for my health and eventually my job. As the day was winding down, I had two more client visits. While I was at the second to last visit my client said to me, " you are sweating profusely." She offered me cold water and said she would call the office and let them know that she was sending me home. I gathered my belongings, quietly thanked her and walked out of her apartment. As I turned to head towards the elevator that I always used to get to the parking lot everything went dark; I awoke to a nurse asking me was I alright. I told her I was fine. She stated, "You can't be! You're lying in the middle of the floor turned opposite of the direction you were originally walking towards." Before I could comprehend what happened the staff jumped into action to make me comfortable. Moments later EMS was surrounding me checking me on the scene. What was immediately determined at the scene was that I was dehydrated. I was taken to the hospital and released a few hours later. The doctors took me out of work for two days with intentions for me to rest.

During the two days of rest I decided to reevaluate where I was in life. I enjoyed my work, but I knew in my heart that I desired more. I knew that I was gifted to do more, yet I was afraid to launch out into the deep. Knowing what you want and having the courage to move forward is not always the easiest process to handle. I knew if I stayed in my comfort zone I would not grow. I may not have fully known what I wanted, but I was wise enough to know that procrastination and stagnation was beneath my God given ability to have an amazing life. God had given me the authority to have a blessed life! I had to trust that whatever my decision would be that I would honor it and push through.

I returned to work still feeling slightly under the weather and wishing that I had more time to figure my life out. I also began to feel pain in my body, joints and started to develop frequent migraines. Four months from the initial fall in June I fell again. This time I was home and was found by my children passed out on the floor in my bedroom. It became obvious that something was brewing in my body. My children were afraid and called 911. Once again, I was told I was dehydrated and that my iron was low; my vitals were normal, and I was given something for pain. This time leaving the hospital was scary for me. I did not feel satisfied with the results and that I had been improperly diagnosed. Something was going on and I felt like my symptoms were indicative of something more. The falls would change the concept of my diagnoses and eventually leave me with a serious situation.

Two months later, in August, I fell again and demanded that further tests be run. My life felt like it was falling apart. My entire body was in pain and at that point I was having trouble walking. My feet were beginning to swell, and I developed migraines, arthritis, & the inability to speak clearly. After several months of hospital trips and doctor's visits, I was finally given a diagnosis, as well as a scare; I was told it was a possibility of cancer. I was not ready for that. As I prayed and talked to God, I made up in my mind that whatever was going to happen I was going to face it with grace. I was going to praise God despite of what I was going through in my life. I had children and grandchildren to raise, parents who were aging, and a career that I loved and was not going to let cancer take me out! I was scared but I knew I had to fight! I knew God had something powerful for me to endure that would shift my life. The shift would ultimately set me up for a win! I could not let a health situation take me out. I had to be strong. I had to fight the good fight of strength and resilience.

By October of 2017, I was a complete mess. I was missing days from work on the weekends because of the pain. I could not get out of the bed. I started to lose weight, my hair started falling out, and I had to depend on my son for everything. My most humiliating moment was when he had to help me shower. My daughters were living in North Carolina and Georgia during that time, yet my son rose to the occasion and took care of me. He cooked, cleaned, gave me my medicine, and prayed for my total healing. He went to all my doctors' visits and became a young man before my very eyes!

During this time my faith increased, my prayer life became mandatory, and the grace of God was everything. Finally, I was given a diagnoses of permanent nerve damage, anemia, arthritis, and low circulation. Apparently, my body suffered an infection that my body had no symptoms of. I carried the infection for eight months, before the doctors could figure it out. It was scary and rough, but I had to praise God for no cancer in my body! Despite my pain, God still allowed me to work and handle my responsibilities. It was not easy and I missed several days from work.

In December of 2017, my supervisor called me into work for a meeting. Even with all that I was going through, she terminated me! In that moment, I trusted in what God was saying to my spirit. He told me to remain strong and not to worry about the loss of my job. He told me He would provide in that moment my soul knew that I had to succumb to the spirit of God. I knew that I had to claim my inheritance. I had to go back to that perpetual Garden of Eden. I had to understand that it was not God's will to live in lack and to spend the rest of my life working for a company that valued my life less that the patients we provided care for. In that moment, God showed me that I was resilient, beautiful, and worthy.

When I was escorted out of the building, I remember thinking my life is in the hands of the most powerful force of creativity on the planet. In me, I had a song. In me, I had a vision. In me, I had the blueprint for a life of success. I had the word of God in my heart. There is no better blessing than what God speaks over your life. God reminded me that He created me and never fails. I had to fully trust God and lean into the lesson He needed me to learn. I did not need to lean into my own understanding - His brilliance was made available in the moment, and simply revealed that I was on my way to create my destiny. In that defining moment, I became who God birthed from the foundation of the Earth. I became the woman who would lead and not follow.

That separation, that threshing, that moment where the enemy wanted me to feel beaten, I felt alive. In that moment I felt the spirit of God telling me that I could release the power that I thought I had over my life and let Him have His way. I had to realize that it was alright to trust God, that He would not leave me or forsake me. Scripture reminded me that God did not give me a spirit of fear, but of sound mind. On the other side of my press would be a testimony so great, that had I not persevered and endured, I may not have believed this story from anyone else. In that defining moment my destiny was greater than my battle. Despite the attempts of the enemy, I was free! No matter what my life felt like, God was preparing me for greatness.

With this new charge to push forward I become more aware of who God created me to be. He created me to be a woman of integrity, honorable, a blessing to my family and others. His desire for my life was to be in position to manifest a beautiful life well lived. I long to one day hear, "well done my good and faithful servant." I was beginning to trust the process and to understand that the final decisions of my life would be contingent upon whatever God desired. I learned fully that I was not my own. I was truly God's handiwork. A picture of His grace in the earth.

This year has proven to be an extended measure of His grace and mercy! Upon returning to North Carolina in January of 2018, I have grown my catering business, Southern Comfort by Carol, I have participated in three anthologies, created a T-shirt line and started an online beauty supply store! As a result of my job loss it forced me to learn about finances, investing and saving money. I had to restructure every area of my life if I was going to bounce back from the trauma that I had faced emotionally, spiritually, financially and fiscally. I had greatness inside of me that needed complete freedom to operate. My challenges and fear forced me out of my comfort zone. I found resiliency in my pain. It is in the darkest most painful areas of our lives that growth abounds! I challenge all of you to grow from those heavy moments in life. It will free you!

I am so grateful that I experienced this part of my life because I am battle ready! When challenges arise, I know how to handle adversity with wisdom and grace. I have learned to encourage myself instead of condemning myself. I have learned to ask for help when necessary and to choose my battles. I have learned my warrior praise and to be in tune with my inner voice. I now know my worth and I will not allow anyone to make me question who I am and my right to be great. I am evolving and loving the woman that this transition birthed. I am appreciating the threshing season in my life. I am deserving of this space of joy and creative ingenuity. I know how to find my way and adapt.

The greatest advice I can give to anyone is to run your own race. Create your ability to master and measure your learning curves. Always give yourself permission to blaze trails, fail if needed, and try again. Your most devastating mishaps in life can change the trajectory of your life and bless you. You never know where failure can take you if you if you internalize it and not move beyond it. Your growth is measured by your strength to overcome. When you acknowledge your failures and make the proactive choice to make appropriate changes, life will give notice and your blessings will overtake you. One thing I know about God, He will provide. What eventually freed me was that I accepted the promises He had for me because I knew they would come to pass. Remember the greater the press, the greater the blessing. Do not keep your testimony to yourself. In your testimony is where your power resides. That power has the audacity to break chains, provides authority in your life and save another woman who desperately needs you and a measure of God given grace. Do not walk away from your sister in her struggle. Trust that if you walk away, karma has a way of finding you when you think you have covered your own sins and iniquities. In your quest to be free, another woman is screaming for her emancipation.

She deserves it just like you when you were seeking change. Another woman who has travelled in pain can identify a warrior cry of another woman who is in pain. It is a cry that does not need to be silenced. It is a cry that needs to be released and rectified through God's anointing. He truly is the only One who can take the band aides of life off and heal you from the inside out. It is advantageous to allow God to heal those wounds so the issues of life cannot reopen them when disappointment enters your personal space. Learning to overcome what previously opened old wounds is the greatest gift one could give to themselves. You cannot heal what you have not exposed. Your ability to share your life shapes what your life becomes. Your charge to your life is paid when you assist another woman in teaching her of her intrinsic value. There is nothing greater than knowing your worth.

We have been given a mantle to uplift and inspire each other. When we ignore that call to action, we do not give ourselves permission to heal and we make it harder to experience God's redemptive grace. I urge any woman who reads this to help another woman in her healing process. I learned how to do that by remembering the times another woman poured into my broken and deteriorating spirit. I refuse to miss out on my blessings because I ignore her plight. Another woman deserves to know that her life can be devoid of pain and misery.

As I bring this chapter to a close, I pray that it finds the woman that it was designed to touch. May this labor of love free her, set her course and bring her faith to fruition. May what I have written break the chains of every woman who is bound.

Kizzie D. Person

Kizzie D. Person was born and raised in a small town called West End in North Carolina. Moore is the county which is famous for its golf and cities of Pinehurst and Southern Pines and PGA tours.

Growing up the youngest of three sisters and being the "baby" of the family, Kizzie spent a lot of time alone. Kizzie's sibling were older and her parents worked many hours, Kizzie took up the hobbies reading, writing and poetry at the tender age of eight years old. She won first place in the Moore County Schools childhood Writing Contest. You can also find some of her poetry accomplishments on the internet. Kizzie D. Person is a graduate of North Carolina Agricultural and Technical State University where she received a B.S. in Computer Technology in 2002. Kizzie is also a stage 3 breast cancer survivor, which leads to many of the testimonies of faith in God. She says to walk by faith in all situations." God will never leave you nor forsake you."

Kizzie currently resides in Greensboro, NC with her three sons.

235

Kizzie's Dedication

In loving memory of my dear mother, Evelyn Person: She has taught me everything she know: how to be strong, depend on Jesus and take everything to the Lord in prayer. She was the backbone, prayer warrior and rock of our family. My mother was like the "glue" of the family; the one who held everyone and everything together who told me continuously to "write a book." Though she is not here in the physical, I know that she is here in the spirit watching over her family. She is at peace.

"Dear mama, see you when I get there."

Connect with Kizzie

Email: kizzieperson@outlook.com

CHAPTER 20
Fighter! Warrior! Conqueror!
#MyLife

As I begin to write my first page, you have no idea what you are about to read or can even visualize what it feels to walk in the shoes of someone with mental illness. Try me; matter of fact, picture this with me.

I am sitting in a small room alone waiting and waiting thinking about how hungry I am and what I must do next, then walks in this short woman with white hair, thick glasses fair skin and a white coat. I am thinking, "ok what is going on?" She sits beside looks me straight in my eyes and says, "I am sorry; you have breast cancer." I sit, frozen with tears running down my face. She hands me tissue and rubs my back, and as she begins to comfort me, she is talking but all I hear is the teacher from the Charlie Brown movies. She hands me a bag full of information and leaves the room. I then exhale!! My heart is beating a thousand beats per second and I burst out in tears and scream! I get my phone and I call my mom! "Mama! Can you hear me? They said I have breast cancer!" She gives the phone to my sister. The next sentence I heard was, "We are on our way up there!" The doctor comes back in, gives me more information about the appointments to come and consoles me as I head for the door. I never wanted to get out of somewhere that fast before; I could feel their eyes watching, knowing that they realized what was going on by the black bag I was carrying. Finally, I made it to the car. It was raining so no one passing by could see the tears of despair, afraid and confusion running down my face. I was in a state of mind with no state of mind; I just kept replaying, "I am sorry you have breast cancer. You have breast cancer" in my head repeatedly. "I think they need to look at those results again because I do not have breast cancer," I resolved in myself.

People like me do not get breast cancer; I have three little boys to raise. They did not even know why my breast was swollen; they said that it was old breast milk, and not once ever did it cross their minds to do a mammogram because of my age. Well I did not think of it either, but still, why did I have to get breast cancer? This is completely undeserved! I do not bother anyone, I mind my business, I am down to earth, everybody likes me — shoot, my name is Kizzie P!! Everybody knows me but I guess none of that matters cause the results remain the same. I have always been taught not to question God but "Why me?" I asked the Lord, because it did not seem fair. Why not give it somebody out here killing and doing bad things or people who do not believe in you? Instead, you give it to me, while they walk on earth, destroy it and take innocent people instead of those who are doing any and everything and living their best life!? Why am I the one that has to end up with cancer?

I find myself spaced out and sitting in my car. My phone rings - my family is on the other end, calling to make sure I am alright and letting me know that they will be there soon. I calm myself down so I can drive home. My boyfriend is at home waiting and I tell him the news. He goes into denial and shock as well; we sit and wait for my family to come. My Mama and my oldest sister come through the door and immediately we all cry and hug each other, and we get into a circle and pray. I then tell them the experience I had, we have dinner and they head back home.

As I sit in a small doctor office known as the oncologist, my family is with me and the doctor comes in sits down and tells me I have stage 3 Invasive ductal carcinoma breast with Her2 positive. We start crying even though we not sure what all of that means only understanding that stage 3 indicates that I have had it for a long time. The doctor tells us the test I must get done because is it possible it could have spread to other parts of my body because of the stage that I am facing. My family and I prepare for what God is going to do, we leave things in Jesus' hands not Man. I come from a Christian, prayer warrior, upon this rock I build my church, tabernacle where we are in the upper room shouting until we fall out, kids go to the back, church family, and I love it! 1 was the one in the back the one who is still flesh and singing "MEET ME THE CROSS ROAD" by Bone thugs in harmony because I am stuck in the world and serving God. Oops! Did I just say THAT? NOW I HAVE BREAST CANCER WHILE ALL MY FRIENDS ARE FREE TO DO WHAT EVER THEY WANT AND I JUST MIGHT DIE!! These are the feelings that overtook my mind. This is the way it is. This is reality and yes, I have faith but who says mine is good enough strong enough? All these things are running through my mind positive and negative, right and wrong, good and bad. I did not know if I was coming or going. I got picked over millions of people in the world to get a disease they some women, and oh yeah, and a small number of men too, but me KIZZIE P, KIZZIE CAPITAL K??! My thoughts continued to consume my faith: "Is my life is over? I'm the pity at the party."

"Ms. Person," "Wake up Ms. Person your surgery is over"!! I had to be put to sleep to put my port in above my left side and my breast; this device made for easy needle access to save the veins in my arms. "Ms. Person, are you in pain?" "Yes," I responded in and out of consciousness to the nurse. She gave me my meds as I wait patiently to leave the outpatient with my family. One thing is for sure you never know how strong you are until you go through something only that makes you stronger. I was not going to let this defeat me! I am a fighter, a warrior a conqueror and this is my life right now. I was going to fight this ugly cancer with God and Jesus on my side till the end. I was finally stepping into a place of war to fight for my full and complete healing.

I sit inside the waiting room, waiting for my name to be called for my first infusion, nervous, scared and ready for this to get over and done. I look around and there are not too many adults in my age group; really, I only see one. Crazy thoughts start running through my head, but I command them to stop. I begin telling myself, "Stop! You do not have time for that! Focus girl! Your life is on the line here." My loved ones are with me for support when they call my name. My buzzer is going off as a nurse is calling me back to the infusion room. I follow the nurse for what seems like this long hall that determines life or death. When I get there, I see people everywhere - some in little private cubicles, some out in the open in chairs hooked with IVs and some in their own room. She leads me to a chair with a cubby and a TV, gets me a warm blanket and asks if I want something to drink or eat, then lets me know that someone would be right with me. I thought to myself, "they make you feel comfortable here." As I wait, my family and significant other talk to me, we go forth in prayer and they ensure me everything is going to be alright. I try to feel the same; my issue is not if I trust God, but I am still flesh so my nerves and mind wander. The nurse comes in, flushes my port and connects the IV and this first time, three-hour journey begins, filled with sleepiness, jitters (they give you something for that). I return home and a friend offers to spend the night help; I felt tired and had a headache, so their offer was well appreciated to say the least. I laid down to rest as her and my significant other helped with kids and myself throughout the night.

The next day I felt fine with had no side effects; God allowed me to wake up without any chemo symptoms to help get my kids ready for school and even drop them off! God is good! That day, not only was I able to complete that task but I was even able to come home, clean up and cook dinner. I take the medicine given to me and I get

240

myself ready for the next chemo treatment which is on the next day. A week or two start to pass and I am not feeling the same; the chemo is making me more jittery, my appetite is going away, my memory is here and there and last night when I woke up, I found hair on my pillow. "Lord I am not liking this. I know the doctor said my hair would fall out, but this early and it has only been two weeks! I am not complaining but just telling you how I feel; there is a difference believe me! Yes, I am thankful to be alive who am I to judge, ?!!" I keep telling myself this as I look in the mirror crying my eyes out and comb my hair only to watch it fall into the sink. Depression starts to sit in as I wonder about my life and why I must go through so much pain when I did not do anything to anyone. "I do not deserve this! What did I do that was so wrong?!" I said while screaming and crying. I get myself together and figure out my next move. I am in warrior mode.

As I sit in the bathroom on the toilet seat my significant other gets the clippers for me; it is time to shave my head. He gets the clippers and starts, and tears run down my face and his, but I am a fighter and a warrior and I can conquer this! MY GOD! My head feels cold and I feel like I look a hot mess with this bald head, so I get a bandana and wrap it up. My kids are young, so I do not have to explain why mommy does not have any hair right now, and I always kept something on my head. Eventually all my hair everywhere fell out. My eyebrows were gone, hair on my legs and arms - yeah everywhere.

One day I had gotten so down I just sat in my car watching the trees blow; I was just trying to hear God because I needed some answers. I did not understand this process I was going through even though I know others go through things but right now. I found myself going through something I felt has no meaning. This piece of folded paper falls from on top of my sun visor. The paper had FAITH written all over it in big letters small letters, diagonal letters just FAITH everywhere. My oldest sister had sent it through the mail as a reminder to me to keep the FAITH, have FAITH. You may not be able to see or understand right now but have FAITH that GOD will heal you. I felt better as I began to have a peace come over me. I knew Jesus would never leave me nor forsake me!!

Eating became harder; all I could drink was orange Gatorade and fast food was out. A person with breast cancer needs to stay out the public and not eat a lot food outside the home or be in crowds. I was feeling good one day and took a risk and went inside one of my favorite stores and the next day I became ill and hospitalized with pneumonia in my right lung and strep throat. I had to stay in the hospital for days! Who knew my immune system was that low and I encounter something like that? My mother and sister came down to make sure I was alright. I ended up going home the day they came. As we were riding in the car, they introduce me to a song that they play all the time, "If He did it before he can do it again." They both start singing and bobbing their heads, "Is this Tye Tribett?", They confirmed as they continued to nod their heads to the music. I laugh and listen to the song and lay back and thank God for my family.

As I sat waiting for the doctor to come in, I thought about all the rounds of chemo I was given, all the injection of steroids because of being HER2 positive and how far I have come. The doctor walks in and explains to me that chemo did shrink the cancer but not enough to save my breast, that it made holes in the cancer that looked like swiss cheese and that the cancer has also spread to my lymph nodes and they are not sure how many. The tears run down my face, the Charlie Brown teacher voice is back and as they rubbed my back, the last thing I hear is that the nurse will be in to get me set up for surgery. I call my family and let them know what's going on.

242

The day of the surgery came, and I had to have a full mastectomy with up to twenty-two lymph nodes cut out. I was nervous and crying, but I had love ones there and the most important Jesus holding my hand. They rolled out into an area where the "team" was ready to put me to sleep. The last thing I remember is when they began asking me questions about my kids, ages and hobbies; before I knew it all I heard was, "Ms. Person. Wake up Ms. Person; the surgery is over." I woke up in so much pain. The nurse already knew from the noises I made and immediately put something in my IV. My legs were numb my chest was wrapped some kind bandage thing; I felt weird and in pain; I have no other words to describe it. I also had these tubes coming out of my chest called drainage tubes!! Pain again!! I am finally rolled back to my room where my family awaited me. The surgeon came in and explained the procedure that was done. My right breast was cut off and 22 lymph nodes removed (basically my underarm has a missing lymph node.) The surgery was a success and they removed all the cancer. Thank you, Lord!! I was too delirious to even know what was going on. I must have stayed a week in the hospital; I later found out that I was done with regular chemo but would have to undergo radiation and more chemo because of being HER2 positive. They told me that since the new chemo was not as strong, my hair would begin to grow back, and I would be on my way to recovery.

As you read this, I hope that you understand what I went through and maybe even why. I do not look like what I been through. My story, I pray, will change your life or the life of someone else; it may even make you understand what it feels like to walk in someone else's mental shoes. But God!! God healed me to show others who He is. **GOD IS THE GREAT I AM** and I am a fighter! I am a warrior! I am a Conqueror! This is who I am; this is MY LIFE!!!

Zulema Nicole Powell

Zulema Nicole Powell was born August 31, 1979. Raised in Queens New York, she attended John Adams High School and took some courses for Criminal Investigations with Everest University. She is the Owner of P.O.P. Destinations and also serves as the founder and C.E.O. of #PushOnPurpose, a T-Shirt line being released in Fall 2019 and Push On Purpose Life Changes U group and individual talk therapy. She always had this type of passion where she just wants to help people, empower them, motivate them, push them to their better, help them birth their dreams and go after the vision assigned to their lives.

Zulema aspires to become a motivational speaker and life coach. She is a Daughter, a Sister, an Aunt, a friend, "thriver", survivor and mother of four young men. Just truly a Nurturer by Nature.

Zulema's Dedication

This is Dedicated to all the women that feel and felt broke, broken, lost, alone, empty, not enough ashamed and as if there is no way out. I am here to tell you that God has not forgot you. He has the power to restore, renew and rebuild each and every part of you. He wants you to trust Him completely and wants you to give Him all of your worries and trust that it is already done. He has created and made us even in time of hardship. He is preparing you for your next level; it is time to nurture the seed that was planted long ago, so you can see the fruit grow blossom and spread. I am not saying anything that I have not experience or endured. So, I can say it with Grace knowing that it is already done. Remember, not everyone is built to go out in the valley endure and come back with the message. I Thank God for choosing me.

To my sons Jayshawn , Zayvon, Zyaire and Zalijay: Thank you for believing in me.

To my niece Destiny: Thank you for always reminding me "Auntie, you are a fighter, you always overcome".

To my second mother, Valarie: You taught me how to pray and trust God on His words; you have been in my corner through it all. Thank you!

To my mother Anglen, "The Camouflage Butterfly": Thank you for giving me life and showing me what strength looks like even when you to fall, and not to look like what you go through.

For My Daddy, the late JP Powell for teaching me early on not just to settle for anything and always telling me "There is nothing you cannot do JZ just go after it".

To my brother, Justin: Thank you for whipping my tears and always listening without judgement.

To my Little Sister, Amani my heart, My Love and first baby: Thank you for being the first one to give me purpose; if it was not for your life I would not be here today.

For my Grandmother, the late Betty A Lynch, My Rock, My Protector, My Wisdom My First Teacher. "My Granny always said, "I do not care how many times you fall - just get back up."

Connect with Zulema

Phone: 919-805-4496

Email: zulemapowell@ymail.com

IG: lifechangesu_blackdiamond

CHAPTER 21

Resting in God's Purpose

My reason my purpose for writing this is because I need to heal and release this. I have a testimony. The adversities of life's experiences have produced purpose within me. Amid the storms that may come or even the ones that have passed I believe that this will help someone else know that they too are not alone. During the time of going through the storms, of not knowing when what or how, my Father showed up and showed me, that YES, I can do all things through Christ who strengthens me.(Philippians 4:13) There is nothing that you will go through or face without His hands keeping you, even when you cannot keep yourself. The statement "you cannot judge a book by the cover" is very true; I do not and did not look like what I was going through or have gone through. I Thank God for that! Praise Him! The appearance of what everyone has seen was not the reality of what was happing in that realm of my life. "She" was good at not looking like her world was falling apart and knew how to smile on the outside and cry like hell on the inside. "She" would carry on conversations while standing in meetings, train new hires, be a happy/good mother and just do and be there to make sure everyone else was ok and ensure that they had no worries. "She" was me and this went on for years. Truth be told I was facing a battle within. I was broke and broken, lost, alone and screaming for somebody to help me. I was at the end of my rope, and at this point, I was crying to hold on. Not realizing I was gone and mentally checked out, I fought to make sense of things to no avail. It was as if there was no identity for who I was. Although I knew who I was for others I could not figure out who I was for ME.

Come walk with me let me take you back for a little while and explain how I lost myself. When I think about it the sad thing is that I was gone before I even got started.

We have all heard the "Once you make your bed you have to lay in it" right? Well, what happens when you lay in a bed that was already made for you but not by you? May I share a little detail about how my God picked me up and showed me how He never took His hands off me and restored my soul and my spirit as I continued to trust Him completely? I did not understand while in the process, but it was all so that I could step into my purpose and to learn the value of one's self and not to ever lose me again.

There I stood homeless - looking in the mirror at the gas station, trying to figure out how I got here what had happened to me. As the tears began to roll down my face everything in my life came to me in a flash. When I looked back over some things, I was so hurt to the core; there I stood, and it was only me. No one came or called, and I felt like I did not exist. All I could say was, "How did this happen? How did I go from everybody's everything for their need and benefit to the girl washing up in the sink at the gas station sleeping in my car at night using a cup to pee in because I was too scared to go to the gas station bathroom late at night. I had already been to the Walmart like a million times throughout the day, but even so, they were no longer a 24-hour location.   I was in complete shock. I stood there and cried and cried because I had always tried to do right and always thought if you do good and be good it will happen for you, but I was way wrong. I had extended me out so much I did not even know who I was anymore, and apparently, nobody else did either or cared.

I found out that people stopped caring when I stopped doing; the moment I stopped being there for them and their needs I became a distant memory if that. For the first time I looked in that mirror and I saw something I did not want to see. I knew that if and when I looked into those eyes, it would be a pain because I had been hidden for so

250

long for so many reasons and had so many issues that I just did not and could not deal with during those times. I forgot what I looked like but, my God, I knew what I felt and to look in the mirror and see those eyes along with everything for what it was borderline unbearable; the pain was sharp and pierced me in a way that I had never felt. As my grandmother would say, "the truth about a person is in the eyes, and the eyes never lie, even when something different comes out the mouth". I stood there wondering why nobody loved me and why did I allow this to happen. Truth be told, I did not even know and wondering if I ever even loved myself. I had been walking around feeling incomplete and as if I was not enough for years and that had become my way of life. Feeling incomplete and not enough came from growing up looking to be acknowledged and validated. I simply wanted to feel like someone truly cared and that I was enough and more. After all of those years of fighting I found myself thinking that I truly was not enough and that this would just be the story of my life. I used to think I was not worthy enough to do or have certain things which is why I always kept pressing. I thought it was my job to make other people happy and that things would be ok for them even if it did not feel like it at the time. This habitual way of life had me in the habit of always overdoing things for people to make sure everyone stayed around. The feeling of knowing that I made a difference peoples' situations made me feel good and served as some type of acknowledgement too (I guess). To me, I felt like others trusted and relied on me and knew if it could be done, I was the one that could make it happen for them.

As time passed, I began giving more of me then I had ever received back not realizing I was losing me each time; I had overcompensated every time. Keep in mind this was my normal. I have done this from the first day I could remember. When you grow up and you see things happening and going on, but your mother still smiles as if

251

everything was perfect, but it was far from perfect, that can become contagious. "My very own Camouflage Butterfly" often reflected, "Just because something is (fill in the blank) you do not have to say it or look like it! Just smile and do not be telling people my business! What happens in here stays in here." So yes, I learned early on before I was ever somebody's mother. I have always sought approval, acknowledgment validation and worked to feel as if I was "enough" from both of my parents. Not to throw either of my parents under the bus, I understand being a parent comes with no instructions, however, a lot has affected me mentally and emotionally. The way I move, talk and deal with people was pretty much how I viewed myself. Think about it: when you are told "your standards are just too high," "you are not realistic," or "just be happy you have somebody" you realize that these excuses become a set up for disappointments and let downs. When a parent chooses their mate over their child and leaves them pushed into motherhood before they have had their children only to be told that they are too grown but had grown people responsibility that is a hard place to be to say the least. To add even more pressure, the infamous words, "you think you cute huh?" or "She always has an attitude! What's wrong with her?" have a way of affecting one's mind and heart. All of these symptoms make for an indescribably painful concoction. I thought to myself, "Yeah, and why not ask what is wrong with you" instead of "what's wrong with her?" I would think when one hears negative stuff all the time one would feel not worthy enough and that their confidence would be shot to hell. You become very timid begin to take on a whole other identity for your protection. There are things that you may want to do or go after but you shoot yourself down because hell, if the ones around you think of you wasting your time or have an opinion about everything you do, but will not even lend a helping hand you will begin to believe what they say and more.

Well, I was counted out before I could start. I was talked about: "Oh she is having another baby? Oh, she is moving too fast! If she does not slow down, she will not make it to 25 years old. How is she going to take care of the kids? I had my little sister before I had my own so the question of how I was going to do it was crazy to me because I took care of my little sister like she was my very own baby. No one jumped in and said, "I will help you, guide you support you mentally emotionally." I did not get that kind of support but became the punchline of peoples' comedy routine and that was fine because I had resolved to protect and love my babies and provide for them by any means necessary. I knew for sure I had to give them what I lacked and did not get. Do not get me wrong I love my mother with my whole life however, my mother was finical. Yes, she provided on the level of things but anything outside of that was another story. Yes, I know she loves me because she is my mother but there is a difference to feel love and know someone loves you because she is the mother. There was no other option; I knew that I had to make sure my sons had the best.

My life shifted gears quickly at that point. I considered about joining the Navy, thinking that if I could do that I would be able to provide for them the right way. Low and behold after sharing my idea I was shot down and the questions began: "Why would you want to do that? Who 'posed to watch them (kids) while you go off? Huh? Hello? You did not think about that did you?" Ok, so my mind was everywhere; I quickly told my family to not worry about it anymore. My brain at that point went into survival mode. I went to the streets and followed the fast money and fast life and you better know that it yielded fast results in my opinion. I never wanted for anything and neither did my sons. Everything they needed they had and anything they wanted they got. Even if I had to do it by myself, I did and did not look back. Still, I walked around feeling like I was

253

not enough, but looked the part and handled it all well. (So, I thought) People were like, "She's about her money!" I had much respect in the street; I was a female on my hustle, and I did not have to run behind, chase guys down nor was I the girl who had to sleep with people to get on. People would say, "Do not cross her because she is not scared, and she does not play", but that too came with a price. I was always the image of the tough city girl who was so strong and had it all together or so people thought. The reality was I had no plan and lived day to day, second by second and never knew what the next day was going to bring. I lived my life high in the clouds. One thing I knew was I wanted my sons to be better than the stereotype of what they said a young, black mother would raise and produce. I just did not know how I was going to do it, but it needed to be different.

I battled myself daily because this was not the life I wanted. I was always looking over my shoulder stayed on guard; I had no relax time or peace of mind but instead it raced constantly as I was always thinking of the next plan "a" or a plan "b" in case something went wrong. Time had continued to go by, years passed, and I still was not where I needed to be. I had got out of the fast life long ago but still, there were battles, and the fact I never dealt with not being enough or worthy. I continued to give of myself until I was completely depleted; I had poured into everyone and everything and had nothing left. I had nowhere to turn and no one to call. Those I had considered to be my reasons to push had all passed away: my Dad first, my sister six months later and then another five days later, my grandmother. I was at a complete lost for words and wanted to give up and let go. My health started to fail me. May 23, 2016, at 37 years old in the hospital I began having mini-strokes, completely lost control of my body fluids and could not talk but seemed like I was having a conversation that would not come out: I did not understanding what was happing to me. I heard that Dr.

Say to me, loudly," Ms. Powell! Ms. Powell not today! Not on my watch! You will not go away from here today! Your heart rate is at 168 beats per minute, your temperature is 105 degrees, you are losing blood, your body is septic, and you are hypothermic Ms. Powell do you understand?" All I could do was look at him because I could not talk. Crazy thing is I heard my grandmother call my name and say, "Tell him what you want." It was like I could feel the whisper of her breath on the rim of my right ear. I looked around and though I did not see my grandmother, I heard her call me loud and clear saying, "Go on and tell him what you want! All you have to do is tell him!"

In my head I am screamed, "God Please help me. I cannot leave my children like this God, please. God, I have to see them off, I have to see them graduate, please!" I started praying as I laid there; fear tried to overtake me as I laid there thinking that this could not be it for me. There I was completely helpless and immobile and unable to move, get up talk or anything; I was literally hanging on to faith. When I saw my sons, I knew I that I could not lay there to die and leave them here my prayer continued: "Lord I have come too far, and I am not giving up now!" I prayed and prayed for fourteen days in the hospital and that seemed like forever. They put me through test after test, GI after GI and more as the doctors worked, trying to figure out what was wrong and how it all happened; the only thing I kept hearing them say was, "She is too young for this." Finally, a turnaround came, and I got to go home. For three weeks after I got out the hospital the doctor called to check on me. He said that in all his years of being in the medical field he had never seen someone in the hands of death, be able to come out and walk away like that. The doctor said, "Ms. Powell I do not know how, but what I do know is God has a plan for you. I am only the doctor and you needed a miracle! Ms. Powell there is a great purpose in your life; He is not done with you yet." I had to stop, think and thank

God for the Grace and Mercy he provided for me when He did not have too. What I have come to realize is that I needed help, it had to be somebody I could trust and that somebody was God. When I look back over my life, He held me when I could not hold myself. It was Him that kept me when I did not have the know-how. So, what I can say is God has always talked to me. What I can tell you now is that I listen and understand.

No one goes through this kind of warfare for no reason. When I look back at what I had to go through I know that there was a purpose in it from the beginning and it was not just for me. I had to surrender to God and trust His will; When the bible says, "It is by faith and not by sight" I can say I live by it. My Father said to me "you do not have to know the why or the how just know it is already done! Yes, I hear your prayers I see the tears. I know you are in pain and I know what you are asking; I will provide you the desires of your heart! Understand my child, it is not in your time but my time. There are going to be some things you have to endure and some things that you are going to have to go through. Yes, there will be some sacrifices required, however, you have to find you even in the midst of the process. I need you to know who you are. I need you to work on you first because I know what I created, and I know what I made. You My child are a blueprint; there is no other you, but you just as you have confidence in others, and you push them for the best I need you to have that within yourself!"

There is a benefit in finding your inner voice. I knew at this point had to trust Him completely and know that He would never leave me; it was evident that, at the breaking point, He always showed up and or sent someone my way! Glory be to God! I had to be better than what was going on around me. I had to rise above my adversity. I had to allow God to sit in my situation trusting that He had what it took to change anything in my life and within me.

Even in the process of writing this book the storms came and tried to knock me down; things that would come out from left to right up and down. I promised myself I would not be defeated. I will not give up; I will not let go of God's promise to me and the fact that He kept me even, when I had nothing in me to move forward.

I owe my God much more than I could ever repay, and today here I stand looking back on the past, the power that my God has and how blessed I truly am. I will not say it was easy, but my God it was worth it; every tear, every let down. If it was not for every adversity, I would not be who I am today. I am not talking about what I look like on the outside, but how I feel on the inside - my internal, mental, faith, and level of confidence I have in me this time. I now understand that when God chose you there is a purpose not just a want. There is a difference in being called and being appointed to what He has for you. Being called does not mean that you have arrived or that there will not be any adversity. Being called does not mean everything will come easy. Being called means, that God is now preparing you, grooming you and getting you ready for what is next; this place literally prepares you for what you have asked for.

(When my Father speaks to me)

Understand my child sometimes it will not be just what you asked for, sometimes it will be what you need. In the process of possessing that need, you will face ups and downs for I need to build you up for what it was that I created and made on the inside of you. People have been trying to put you where you do not belong. You can never place a square in a circle for it will never fit.

My child you had to learn how to push past the pressure and know that deception, distraction and doubt will try and steal your joy and your destiny for they all have been after

257

you for a long time; that is why the adversity continued to come in the way that it was coming. You had to go through a state of transition; when people show you who they are believe it. You was in a season of where you just tried to help and save everyone and that was not you job.

In the process along the way you forgot who you were and what your path was to be. You allowed all that you desired to be put to rest, and I could no longer allow you to move on the path in which you was going. So yes I has to take you down under the water, so you know who it was and being you closer to me.

Me: I know understand on a different level that my God has been calling me for a long time. I realize that yes there was reasons for going through all that I have endured. God had me in the process so that the purpose can be birthed. My father in Heaven knows that when He created me, He had placed some gifts deep down in the inside that was is a perfect image of Him. He knew that one day they will flourish and grow. Thank you Father for just simply choosing me and knowing I am worthy.

(My father says) — I am going to use all of the gifts that I have stored up within you. I am going to use you through your vision the prophetic the prophecy, yes, for there are some things you can see and have insight on. Your voice, because of the mighty power down in you, projects in a way that will grab the ones that I to need to reach. You, my child, have what it takes. It is not what you look like or about you fitting in with other missionaries. It is about being able to give the Word and break it down so other will understand on the level that they are on and bring them even higher in Me. I know you can deliver it just as how I bring it to you. Yes, there is a difference between Process and purpose and my child you have been in the process for the greater of your purpose. Now it is time for your promotion.

Centoria Robertson

Centoria Robertson is a mother of one precious baby girl and successful entrepreneur. Born in Reidsville, North Carolina and raised in various cities, she now resides in Charlotte, North Carolina. A true businesswoman, she has been blessed to become an Accountant, Certified Tax Instructor (2013) and C.E.O. and founder of Golden Locust, Inc., which houses an array of products and services. In 2017, Robertson received her B.A. in Accounting and has accomplished several certifications in this field. She started her blog almost two years ago, after being diagnosed with a health condition and her daily walk, which are both near and dear to her heart. Along with all that she has accomplished, she is also working on her solo book and other projects as well!

Centoria's Dedication

To every person who knows their identity but battles with not living out their identity and the truth of who they really are: I pray that my testimony gives you the push you need to be your best you and all that you are called to be.

Connect with Centoria:

Email: Glinc3@icloud.com

CHAPTER 22

Identity Without an Identity

My mom has told me that, since I was a little girl, she immediately recognized I was very wise from the very moment she looked me in my eyes on the day she birthed me, and the nurse put me in her arms. She said "I just knew! You had an old soul about you; I have always known." I was born and raised a church girl. I was tarrying for God at the age of five or six years old. Nobody, I mean nobody in my family, or the church told me I had to, talked me into it or forced it on me. No, no, no! I have had a heart for God since before I can remember. One day, a close friend and I, while talking, reminded me of how I had ministry in me as a kid. She said that I would minister to them (my friends and schoolmates) at school. I mean, I did not know it was ministering at the time - I just mostly spoke on right and wrong. You know how kids are, they curse and fornicate and do other things that we should not do as adolescence or even as unmarried adults. I promise I am not judging at all; I am just simply speaking according to God's Word and how we are to live. (Trust me, I may have not been having sex, smoked, or cursed but I did my little dirt.) Coming up and even now, I do not talk much. Generally, if I know you personally that becomes a different story; I can talk with you from sunup to sundown. I must add that it must be something I am interested in talking about or something that I can engage in. There is one thing that I really do not like and that is gossip! All my life I had to deal with people not understanding me when I talked "deep". They would say that I was crazy, that I did not know what I was talking about and so on. I still get that even now and I would say more than ever.

Growing up we lived in the country called Browns Summit, North Carolina; at the time, it was four of us, three girls and one boy, I was the "middle" child. All of a sudden, ten years later from when my younger sister was born, my parents became pregnant with our fifth sibling, a fourth girl, the baby girl of our family and so at that point, it became five kids. I was REALLY the "middle" child at that point. When you are the middle child, you are basically ignored. Our home was down a long dirt road that led into a cul-de-sac of 3 houses. Our home was in the middle. We lived on about a half an acre of land where my mom and dad grew vegetables in two fields and we were surrounded by fruit trees, oak trees, pear trees, walnut trees, blackberry bushes, persimmons trees, and apple trees just to name a few. My parents had started their own gardens. One part of the field was strictly corn and the garden was halved by a huge apple tree and a bed of blackberry bushes running along on each side of the tree, which was perfectly centered in the field. On the other side of the field, the garden was filled with tomatoes, cucumbers, squash, green beans, okra, peppers, zucchini and so many other kinds of vegetables. It was great. Understand that my parents were not rich pertaining to money but, we were rich in love and in nourishment. We had an amazing life, a blessed life and were happy children for the most part. My mom and dad provided everything they could for us. We would always have an amazing time making up games and being able to venture out. We also had our times of the typical sibling rivalry "thing". We were surrounded by nothing but trees and we had a creek behind our home. There were trails in the woods where we would walk and just play and discover new plants and trees. Trust me, times were not always good; however, the good outweighed the bad, always. When I think about my childhood and where we lived, we literally were surrounded by a Garden of Eden.

Prior to my baby sister being born, when I was about ten or eleven years old give or take, my siblings and I were outside playing in the front yard having fun. I do not remember who brought it up, I believe it was my oldest sister; she asked, "Let's go around and everybody tell what they want to do when we grow up." Went in order from oldest to youngest. So, my older sister says "I am going to be a fashion designer/stylist", my brother says "I am going to play professional ball", I say "I am going to be an attorney", and my younger sister said "I am going to be a doctor". When I gave my answer, my siblings got excited and agreed with me. They said things like "Oh yeah, you would be a really good lawyer. You're very aware of things and you have the ability to pick up on things that no one else does, you ask questions that no one ever thinks to ask, you pay attention to detail, you can pick up on when a person is not telling the truth, you are really good at debating, and you can talk." We all began to laugh. We all supported and encouraged one another — that was just the nature of our relationship. Each one of us seemed to have a pretty good understanding of who we were. We were smart, some smarter than others and I must say myself that I am not talking about me. My siblings are very smart, and I am one who can happily say that with no grudge, jealousy, or anything of such. At the age of five I was diagnosed with a medical condition called Sickle Cell Anemia that affects the blood and immune system. Then, at the age of eighteen, I was diagnosed with a medical condition called Psoriasis that affects the skin. I have always been artistic. My artistry was nurtured at a very young age. My mom taught us that just because we had a disability did not mean we could not do things; we could do anything we put our mind to, we just had to do it a different way.

As I said before, I grew up in the church. I was raised in and by my grandma's church family on top of my blood family. My grandma was heavily involved in church so it was natural that we (my siblings & I) would too. My grandma eventually became president of the usher board, I was around seven or eight at the time; she recently stepped down this past year. (Remember, I am thirty-eight now.) Most of our days and time was spent in church. If the church doors were open, we were there. Due to the level of my grandma's involvement, that only led to us being just as active. I was on the junior usher board and in the junior children's choir. Then eventually, once I got older and reached a certain age, I went from junior usher board to teen to adult and from junior choir to adult choir. My love for God and serving Him and seeking Him was my everything. I loved to sing, and I could really sing. I learned starting from being in the church junior choir. I also loved writing. I wrote poems and journaled all the time, everyday even. I also loved to dance. All these things I still love and some I do, while others I want to get back to doing them someday. They are a part of who I am. By the time I reached high school in '95 by my senior year in '99, I was not sure of exactly what it was I wanted to do. I had always wanted to take the debate course and join the debate team but, I pursued other interests. I was in NJROTC, Dance, and Manager for the Varsity basketball team and some other courses I chose to take. I had always wanted to take dance lessons since I was about four or five years old. The only thing that kept me from taking them was because my parents could not afford to pay for them. I was not able to pursue any extracurricular activities for that very reason. The "wise" part of me understood and was okay with it. I was excited, happy, and thankful to learn that it was available to me when it was. And even though I really did want to be an attorney, once I learned I would be in law school for a long time I decided against it. I believe it was about 20 years at that time or at least it felt like it would be! I did not like school at all. At the time, I just wanted to go because everybody made it seem like college was "the only way to go" next after high school. When it came to career paths and the road that had to be taken, the only next route to take was college for me, so I thought. At the time, I was the first one to go to college between my oldest sister and brother. So, I went to NC A&T State University and I majored in "UNDECIDED"; I took Computer Science courses. That was my first semester, my second semester I changed to Electronics Computer Technology. Initially, I wanted to major in Dance. I had the support of my instructor, she even talked to the Head the dance department at A&T without me even knowing. But, one day I was talking with a family member on the phone and they asked had I chose a major yet. I remember telling them that I had a passion to dance and that is what I wanted to major in. They told me that they felt like dance was not a promising career path and that I needed to go for something else. From that moment on, I was crushed; this "advice" came from a person I highly respected and valued their opinion as well. At that time in my life I only knew to respect my elders and like I said before, I just really respected and valued their opinion. I looked up to a lot of people in my immediate and extended family so much so, that whatever they taught me I took it as face value and nothing else. That is how I am period. So, I just threw dance out as an option and I have only danced once since then. The spring semester of my second year I got sick and had to withdraw from school per my doctor's orders.

I also worked while I was in school, high school and college, but church was put in the back seat. I was not involved as much, and I did not attend as much. Once I was withdrawn from school, I just worked. Once I started college, I kept the job I had in high school and I got a second job which was Telemarketing. Then I moved to Customer Service and did that for thirteen years. I understood afterwards that trying to do all of that led to getting very ill and having to withdraw. I attempted to go back to school a couple times, however, every time I would begin to have serious health issues. From the time I started college, I did not know what I wanted to do. I was interested in so many things, but I always felt like I could only pick one. I knew and understood that I did not want to, I just felt compelled to. I knew and understood since I was very young that I felt something in me that just felt so much bigger than me. I knew God called me to do some things and I wanted to do them, but I did not know how to go about it; I did not know one person who had taken that route and could mentor me. I knew I was called to be a Motivational and Inspirational Speaker. I wanted to act, be an author, dance, and model. I really did not know how to go about getting the ball rolling, how to get into doing these things without school (in my mind) and I was having to take a back seat with school. I was put in the situation of, either go to school and not have health care or work a job that provided healthcare. I had to choose the job with healthcare. For so many years I struggled with the things that I really wanted to do that was near and dear to my heart. I allowed the enemy, myself, and others to keep me from doing the things I really wanted to do. Despite my path one thing I learned was this: when God has called you to do something and you have the heart to do it, He is working behind the scenes even the more to make it so. I felt for a long time that I was doing things wrong when I initially thought I was doing the right things. When things turned for the bad, I always thought I did something wrong somewhere along the journey. I thought "I just had to have done something." In my mind, that could be the only reason things were going the way they were. I was getting sick all the time, had to withdraw from school and had to go back home a few times. My jobs were affected, and I was feeling like I was always the person to lend a helping hand and be there for loved ones even when I could not help myself but when the roles were reversed no one was to be found.

I felt that way until about 10 years ago. I was about 28 years old and one day I had reached my breaking point. I fell to my knees in tears and all I knew to do was to call out the wonderful Name, JESUS, and that is what I did. I was fed up, tired, and deeply hurt. I had gone through life being a true child of The Most High. I treated people the way I wanted to be treated and yet people abused my kindness and took it as weakness; all of this also affected my health. The psoriasis flared up when I got to college. Imagine a young eighteen-year-old girl, literally breaking out with dry patches all over her body! Imagine a girl just leaving high school, starting her college journey and having to deal with a blood disorder at the same time. I was crushed but, I did not break. I had an amazing support system with family and friends that did not allow me to go crawl into that dark hole and not come out. That is what I wanted to do deep down inside, go hide, but Gods power, Holy Spirit in me was so strong that it would not allow me to do so. I was not perfect but, I kept God at the forefront and I always tried to do the right thing. I did not complain, I embraced whatever was thrown my way. Sickness, unable to go to school, unable to work, etc. In that break down, the Lord gave me a revelation. The Lord had taken me back ten years, exactly, when I was eighteen years old going off to college, a young girl innocent and pure and not really knowing how to express what she wanted. Each flash was a major moment that happened from the age of eighteen. It told the story of how God had to take me through the things I went through to get me to where He had me right there in my bedroom floor sobbing. The revelation was this: He created me in His image, in His likeness and to Him I was perfectly imperfect. He showed me how it was Him who put all those things on my heart and made me to be "different", one of His chosen. He helped me understand that that was the very reason why I was the black sheep in my family; that because I go so hard for Him and I speak His truth, the majority of people would not understand or "get" me or where I was coming from with the God Knowledge I had. He told me that I already had what I needed to do what He put in me. He appointed and anointed me to be a writer, a poet, an author, a speaker, a healer, a teacher, an encourager, an inspirer, an accountant, a lawyer, an actor, and a dancer - all I needed to do was put in the necessary work and get started with doing the work! He told me that He was going to guide me through it all and be right there with me through it all. On that day, I graduated in Heaven. The Lord had been waiting on me, He needed to get me in the place of understanding that I needed to put Him FIRST; not just keep Him at the forefront because that is not where He belongs in our lives. The forefront can become the middle front, the last front, nor the in between front. We are to put Him first and keep Him there and what really matters is the spiritual; none of this fleshly stuff. That day God took me higher in Him, I got moved up a level in the Spirit that day. I did not take it lightly either. I literally went from "girl of religion" to walking in my true spiritual being self that I already had been, I just did not know it until that day back in June 2013. My face turned fully to and on God at that very moment in my bedroom and I have not been the same since. While the Lord blessed me with the revelation of who He had created me to be, He was taking me through some trials, storms and rains, valleys and up rugged mountains and hills to strengthen me, heal me, supply me with another level of knowledge and wisdom to help me get to the place of knowing for sure that yes, I was hearing Him all along the way. Now, another story for another time is what has happened over these last ten years that has kept me from where I should be in this moment. Well according to God, I am right where I need to be. I would always have to remind myself of that because I would get on myself about how I went about things and how much time I wasted; this tactic was nothing but the enemy. God delivered me from that recently this year.

I pray that, from this writing, you capture a few truths that you can apply now and for the rest of your life. When it comes to doing you and being the best version of you, do not second guess, constantly question, listen to others and their opinions, or ignore what God put in you to do; if it comes in your mind and makes your heart race and flutter in a good way, that is Holy Spirit telling you what to do. Reject procrastination; do not just sit on it like I did, but instead, get up and go do it. Make sure you are doing it with a pure heart not looking for anything in return, especially money, because God is going to supply every need - He just needs us to get in position and do our part to the best of our ability. For those who received more than what I have just shared I trust that it is something good and positive; for me, that is all that matters, and I give God all the glory and praise for it. Praise be to God that He already know what is going to happen and when it is going to happen. He did not lose faith in me as I went through my process; it was me who lost faith in Him. Today, my love in and faith for God is stronger than ever before and I continue to grow in Him every day.

Christian Renae

Christian Renae is a 37-year-old author, entrepreneur, strong, independent and determined vessel. She is a native of Canton, Ohio but was raised in the Washington, DC, Virginia, and Maryland area and now resides in North Carolina.

Christian has worked in education for the past seven years and worked in the healthcare field ten years prior.

She is a loving and devoted mother of five children (three boys and two girls to be exact), overcomer, future millionaire, lupus survivor and kidney disease survivor who has knocked on death's door more than once.

Christian is a woman who chooses to live her best life regardless of any circumstance that life may bring her way.

Christian's Dedication

To my parents: James for giving me a loving spirit and Vanessa for giving me a fighting spirit.

To my children, Aaron, Shiloh, Tahj, Christiona and Nadia: without you guys my life would be boring!

To my Auntie (Stephanie) for being my very best friend!

To my Dell'e Pop, Erica, Lisa, Wanda and Penny for always being my clear mind and ear when I needed you.

To Pastor Johnson and Dr, Michele Johnson for lighting a fire that will never burn out.

And to my family and friends:
Each one of you hold a very dear place in my heart that I cherish dearly!

Connect with Christian
Email: cturnercanton57@gmail.com

CHAPTER 23

Touching the Hem of His Garment

She felt cut off from God and man.
Then Jesus came into town (the room)
She believed if she could touch the hem of his garment
that she would be healed.
So, she prayed and cried as she reached for his garment
(she touched him) and he touched her too, more deeply
than she ever imagined...

Imagine being twenty-nine years old, never been sick, living your life, raising your children, working, and going to school, enjoying the life and doing what any healthy normal twenty-nine-year-old would do and having all of that change in a matter of two weeks! One day while working nightshift at a nursing home, I started to feel a little headache and decided to ask the nurse for some medication. I am normally a person that is against taking medicine for headaches; I would rather deal with a headache than taking a medication to help ease the pain. This headache was too much and I could not function, let alone get my job done. When morning came, I went home to get my children to school, and on to my Biology class I went. I could not miss class because we were testing, and I could not miss the test. When I was able to finally get home and relax, things did not get any better. My chest was hurting, and my body was feeling a way that I could not bear (mind you that I had four of my children naturally). I went to the hospital and they diagnosed me with having a UTI and pneumonia; they kept me for a day or two and sent me home with medication. Days later after returning to work and back to school, my symptoms were not getting any better.

I had gotten to the point where everything in my body was hurting. That day when I got home, I laid in my bed and did not move for the next two days. I remember my oldest child, who was ten or eleven at the time, coming to check on me. I can remember telling him "yes" and sending him on a task to tell his dad; these moments would be me asking him to get me something to eat or drink. Upon one of his returns back into my room, I heard his voice echoing in my head, "Mommy are you okay? Mommy are you okay?" I would always tell him "yes" and that I just need to rest, but this time was different. I heard a real concern in his voice, I got up and things did not look the same. My body felt so weak. I had a picture of a woman kneeling in prayer on my bedroom wall; when I looked at the picture of that woman, I felt like it was me. I remember telling my children's father, who was my husband at the time, that it was time for me to go to the hospital.

Before leaving the house, I must have blacked out a couple of times. I remember walking down the stairs but not all of them; I do not remember getting in the car, but I remember undoing my seatbelt before getting out the car to enter the hospital. My children's father got me a wheelchair to go into the hospital. I can remember him rolling me to the counter and the desk clerk asking me for my social security number; I do not remember making it beyond the first three numbers. I completely blacked out only remembering bright flashing lights coming from above my head. I was transferred from one hospital to another and woke up days later in a hospital; no one knew where I was, not even me. I had been transferred because the one that I was originally admitted to was not equipped to handle my condition and my body did not respond to their treatment. When I finally woke up and gained some knowledge of who I was and where I was, I used the room phone to call home. When my children's father answered the phone, I asked him where he was because the last thing I

272

remembered was that he was right there with me. I was taken by surprise when he asked me where I was: "What do you mean where am I, you dropped me off here?" I exclaimed. He replied, "I called the hospital, they said that you were not there, and they didn't know where you were." I was so upset with him at first. I thought to myself, "how in the world are you going to let these people tell you that I am not in their hospital, and they didn't know where I was, and why didn't you shut the place down until they found me? Better yet, why didn't you look for me?" We later found out that my face, lips and eyes were so swollen that they thought he had beaten me. It was then that I found out that I was in congestive heart failure.

I was in Step down ICU so everyone that came into my room had to be gowned and masked. The doctors ran all kinds of tests: my heart, my lungs and my kidneys were shutting down all at once and I was in septic. But why? I heard all kinds of illnesses. Could it be hepatitis? No. I worked in healthcare and took the medication to prevent it and took the test to make sure the shots worked. Could it be HIV? I had one doctor that just knew that was it. My response was "I get tested every year and I've never had a bad report," yet my mind still wondered. I thought about the people that I had slept with, and the people that my children's father slept with as well. Then we finally had an answer - Dr. Fletcher at Wake Forest Baptist Hospital was able to put the pieces together. He told me, "Christian we believe that you have Lupus." I replied, "Lupus? What is that?" Lupus is a systemic autoimmune disease that occurs when your body's immune system attacks your own tissues and organs. Inflammation caused by lupus can affect many different body systems — including your joints, skin, kidneys, blood cells, brain, heart and lungs. Lupus can be difficult to diagnose because its signs and symptoms often mimic those of other ailments[4]. Fear began to grip my mind. I have never heard of this! What does this mean? Am I dying?" The doctors put me on high doses of steroids and a medication that is used to treat patients who have received a transplant. The medications were working, and I was able to leave the ICU.

My mom started noticing changes in my behavior and in my mental status especially when I began talking "outside of my head." I was obsessed with me dying. I talked about it so much some doctors thought that I wanted to die or could possibly kill myself. I would get my food tray and it would have an expiration date but was abbreviated with "exp"; I thought that it was the time that I was going to die. I remember anticipating my death and would go to sleep. When I would wake up, I would always ask or tell my mom, "I'm still here?", and she would always respond, "Yes Chris! Where are you supposed to go? If God wanted you, He would have taken you." There is something about a mother's love.

The mental episodes kept happening, but no one knew why. The doctors told my mom that I may have always been like this and what ever happened just made it come out more. There was even a time that I posted a video on Facebook of me talking crazy but did not remember doing it. The doctors sent in different psychologists to talk to me; I told one that he was the devil. They wanted to put me in a mental ward, but I thank God that my mom was there and was able to talk and fight on my behalf. She figured out that it had to be from something that the doctors had given me; we later discovered that the culprit was the steroids. The steroids also made me gain almost 80 pounds in water weight. I went from 125 soaking wet to 205 pounds. During the duration of my hospital stay the only thing that calmed

---

4 www.mayoclinic.org

me was listening to gospel music. *Let Me Touch You* by Kirk Franklin was my favorite song and I played that song over and over. When the music played at night, it seemed that I would always wake up to hear that song. I knew that God was going to bring me out and that He was going to heal me. One time my mother and I went on a walk to one of the hospital rooftops. When I saw the sun, it seemed like it was the brightest sun that I had ever seen, I laid down on the ground and told my mom that the sun was going to heal me.

After a 30-day stay, I was able to return home to my children, just in time for my youngest child's birthday who turned six years old. I thank God for my then church family. They made sure that my home and children were taken care of. My children gained a mother, Mrs. Sharon, who would watch them and keep them like they were her own. Me being a momma I tried to make everything was normal for my children. I felt that they were too young to understand everything that their momma had gone through. How do you tell children that their mother was almost taken away from them forever? This was one of the main reasons that we kept their visits short and sweet when they visited me at the hospital.

I stayed out of work for close to a year while I took time to take care of me. I read up on lupus and I wanted to know everything about it. I learned that it effected mostly African American women starting as young as age fourteen. I went on a mission to educate people about lupus. While planning one of my events and taking a medication called Bactrim for a UTI, my body was under attack again. I was not feeling too well so my mom told me to go lay down and take a nap. I checked my blood pressure and discovered that it was very high. I kept asking where my ex was (he was out doing his thing). When I called my friend Wanda, she did not think I sounded right; she knew something was wrong with me and came to the house to see me. She found me sleep in my bed and was unable to wake me up. I had a grand mal seizure and was found and unresponsive in my own bed. Here I was sick and in the hospital for duration of time again, and after countless tests, they discovered that I had fluid on my brain. There I was, reaching for the hem of Jesus' garment again, knowing that He would take care of me. Time went on and the fluid went away.

Now I am thirty-seven and still living my life and thanking a loving God that I am still here. Every day is not easy; I still fight battles with my health. I often find myself thinking how I almost did not make it to see my thirtieth birthday and how I have gone through more in my life up to this point, then most people would go through in their whole entire lifetime. I am still seeking and pressing my way to touch His garment.

Brandi L. Rojas

Wife I Mother I Pastor I Author I Mentor I Entrepreneur I Visionary Author

Pastor Brandi L. Rojas is a native and resident of Greensboro, N.C. She serves with her Husband, Pastor Omar Rojas at Maximizing Life Family Worship Center in Greensboro, N.C., a vision God birthed through them in 2015. Rojas has been in Dance Ministry for over 20 years and is a 2009 graduate of the School of Disciples taught under the late Bishop Otis Lockett, Sr. Pastor Rojas was licensed to preach the Gospel on February 27, 2011 in Thomasville, N.C., and as a result DYmondFYre Global Ministries was born. Rojas was ordained as an Ordained Elder June 2012, was installed as Pastor with her Husband, Pastor Omar Rojas in January 2013 and now serves as Executive Pastor for the vision God has assigned to them through #MaxLife.

Since that time, she and her Husband, also known as #TeamRojas, by God's mandate, have been honored in the marketplace and birthed several evangelistic causes. In 2013, Rojas was named Sweetheart of the Triad, an award given based on community involvement. In January 2014, Rojas opened FYreDance Studios and Liturgical Arts Consulting which provides on-site instruction, virtual teaching, consultation services, choreography services and deliverance and healing dance encounters. In that same year, after serving with Pastor Cassandra Elliott and The Gathering Experience for two years, she began serving and currently serves as the Lead Dance Vessel Coordinator for this time of worship amongst those who are hungry, thirsty and desperate for the presence of God. The following year a prayer walk initiative was created to bring the local churches and community together to work together and help lead the lost to Jesus Christ and empower the world through a vehicle called The Gatekeeper's Legacy; she has also served as part of the planning and leadership committee for the National Day of Prayer for the City of Greensboro and currently serves as the youngest committee member, only African-American and only female on the core team.

In February 2016, Rojas launched out again to begin The Legacy Ladies Fellowship, an organization created to help women of God pray, push and live the reality of what God has called them to do. Most recently to this list of mandates, The CrossOver Resource Center was added, working to provide solutions for life's transitions to the community. Rojas released her first book in June 2016 entitled In the Face of Expected Failure and her sophomore project, Humpty Dumpty in Stilettos: The Great Exchange, in November 2016. It was with the second book release Fiery Beacon Publishing House was launched, serving current and upcoming authors, playwrights, poets, blog writers and more. Humpty Dumpty in Stilettos was nominated for the national Literary Trailblazer of the Year Award in June 2017 by the Indie Author Legacy Award in Baltimore, Maryland and in July 2017 she was noted as an International Best-Selling Author for her part in a collaborative effort called Stories from the Pink

Pulpit: Women in Ministry Speak. Rojas is also a two-time nominee for Trailblazer of the Year, Choreographer of the Year and Women of Inspiration with ACHI Women Supporting Women, Inc. She is currently preparing for her next solo release, Rehobeth Church Road: Suicide in the Pulpit and is celebrating the first publishing company collaboration for Fiery Beacon Publishing House entitled, When Legacy Arises from the Threshing Floor: A Collective of Trials and Tribulations Superseded by Undeniable Triumphs!

In the Marketplace, Pastor Rojas is also known for her progressive efforts through her travel company, DYmondFYre Destinations and the international platform of Surge365 where she makes it a priority to share the reality and necessity of multiple streams of income which empowers the home, community, nation and world. Pastor Rojas is grateful and humbled at how God continues to expand the entire vision, not just to the United States, but internationally as well.

#Team Rojas are the proud parents of five children. Pastor Brandi Rojas is a Worshiper, Servant, Praise Vessel, and Prayer Warrior, but most of all, she is a vessel who is on fire for God.

Wife I Mother I Pastor I Author I Mentor I Entrepreneur I Visionary

Maximizing Life Family Worship Center

https://www.facebook.com/MaximizingLife/

Phone: (336) 497-1897

Fiery Beacon Publishing House (Consulting/Publishing Group)

https://www.facebook.com/FieryBeaconCPG/

DYmondFYre Destinations

https://www.facebook.com/thelegacybuilder/

The Legacy Ladies Fellowship

https://www.facebook.com/LegacyLadiesFellowship/

Phone: (302) 404-3973

IG and Twitter: @allthingsdymondfyre and @maxlifedfg

Please connect with the awesome and dynamic women in this literary work through their contact information listed in each chapter. From the grips of abortion, molestation, divorce, mental anguish, low self-esteem, abuse and even death they have escaped!

Every single one of these women:

Jesta, Laura, Mary, Andrea, Janelle, Ciltona, Dominique, LaRissa, LaTasha, Brigitte, Sharon, Queena, Rose, Rolonda, Patrice, Shereka, Melanie, Gresha, Carol, Kizzie, Zulema, Centoria, Christian and Brandi have become Legacy, The One that Arose from the Threshing Floor!

"27 The satraps, the prefects, the governors and the king's counselors gathered around them and saw that in regard to these [wo]men the fire had no effect on their bodies—their hair was not singed, their clothes were not scorched *or* damaged, even the smell of smoke was not on them."

Daniel 3:26-27 (AMP)

Made in the USA
Columbia, SC
01 November 2019